Enjoying Ballet

Whether you know a lot, a little or nothing at all about ballet, this book will help you to understand it better and enjoy it more. The author traces the historical background of ballet and explains how dance, drama, music, costumes and scenery combine to make a whole. She describes some of today's great dance companies and most popular ballets and gives biographies of the dancers you may see performing. You can also find out what it's like to be a pupil in one of the top ballet schools and read how famous dancers of past and present started their careers.

Jean Richardson writes books and articles for children and adults. She has been going to the ballet since she was very young and has a large collection of books on the subject.

Enjoying Ballet

Jean Richardson

With a Foreword by Anthony Dowell, CBE

Beaver Books

First published in 1977 by
The Hamlyn Publishing Group Limited
London · New York · Sydney · Toronto
Astronaut House, Feltham, Middlesex, England
Reprinted 1978

© Copyright Text Jean Richardson 1977
ISBN 0 600 31412 X
Printed in England by Cox & Wyman Limited
London, Reading and Fakenham
Set in Linotype Pilgrim

Contents

Acknowledgements

The publishers are grateful to the following for
permission to reproduce photographic material:
Zoe Dominic – Plates 5, 6, 9 and 11; EMI Film
Distributors – 10; The Mansell Collection – 1
and 2; The Royal Ballet – 8; Leslie Spatt – 7;
The Victoria and Albert Theatre Museum – 3;
Reg Wilson – 4.

Foreword

If ballet is to thrive we need not only good dancers, but good audiences too. Not just large audiences (though this is vital), but audiences who know what ballet is about and who know whether what they are seeing is good or bad. I hope that this book will help to produce a steadily growing audience for ballet.

Never before has ballet been so popular or available in so many forms and so many places. Sixty years ago ballet could only be seen in this country when Diaghilev brought his Ballets Russes on a visit. Now we have at least six important companies in Britain, and four of these base their programmes on classical technique. This doesn't, of course, mean that they dance only the 'classics' – they often use classical technique to express very modern ideas and themes.

This book will give you an idea of how those of us who are dancers live. It is a strange, concentrated life, demanding strong discipline. I learnt my first steps at the age of four. My mother was very keen that my sister should learn to dance, and she was sent to a school that offered not only academic subjects, but also ballet, character and modern dance (or, as it was then called, musical comedy). As it was convenient for my parents to have us both at the same school, I was sent along too when I was old enough. I enjoyed moving to music very much, and was extremely lucky to have the opportunity to dance on a 'real' stage so early in my life.

It was at the Fortune Theatre, in London's Drury Lane, while taking part in our annual school display, that I caught the intoxicating 'bug' of the theatre. I had no great desire or ambition to become a ballet dancer, but knew already that I had to be a part of this make-believe world and that it would be through my dancing that I could enter it.

At sixteen I realised for the first time how physically demanding my future career was to be. This was quite a shock, as when I was very young everything came easily to me and at times I had found dancing very boring. I now had to face up to the fact that a great deal of stamina had to be built up, and I would have to start the never-ending search for personal satisfaction in perfection of movement.

It is easy to moan about hard work, and I half believe that the audience should not have to realise this. But on the other hand I am very glad that more people now know what goes into the making of a classical dancer, for I still find it hard when the male ballet dancer is made fun of (sometimes successfully) by clowns and comics. We are a combination of athlete, actor and dancer, but differ from athletes in that we may never show strain or exhaustion, even at curtain calls! The great part of our work is done off-stage, during 'class', rehearsals, learning new roles and learning new ballets. What you see on the stage is just the tip of the iceberg.

I hope you will spend some happy hours with this book, and that it will help you to enjoy your visits to the ballet. The more you know about it, the more you will enjoy it.

1·What's it all about?

You don't have to want to be a dancer or particularly like dancing yourself to enjoy going to the ballet. After all, you don't have to be a tennis champion to enjoy Wimbledon, or much of a gymnast to recognise the talent of the girl who won all those gold medals at the Montreal Olympics. Most of us will never be much good at activities that require great physical skill and hours of training and dedication, but we all have the same bodies – arms, legs, and muscles – as athletes and dancers. And part of the thrill we get from watching them comes from the way in which they can do things that the rest of us can only dream of. Even the most earth-bound people can be dancers in their imagination, and one of the great pleasures of ballet is that it is able to express feelings such as love, grief, happiness, excitement, in the kind of movements that we recognise as being just right.

If you haven't seen a ballet yet, you may not have realised that dancing and ballet are not quite the same thing. People have always loved dancing and used it to express all kinds of things. Many folk dances go right back to ancient times and are part of fertility rites. Folk dancing still takes place all over the world and has made its contribution to ballet, but its roots and aims are very different. As we shall see, ballet began in a very special world, and dancing is only one part of what is involved.

Although you can sometimes see ballet on television or at the cinema, it is first and foremost live theatre. It should properly begin with sitting in a theatre – if possible a beautiful one with rows of boxes and lots of gold paint and red plush, like some of the great opera houses – listening to the orchestra tuning up. Of course you may be somewhere much less grand, but it is worth remembering that ballet began as an entertainment for kings and always looks at home in a beautiful building. The feeling of glamour was considered so important to the success of the Russian ballet when they visited Paris (you can read about this in Chapter 4), that on the first night the manager filled the front row of the dress-circle with beautiful women. He gave tickets to the loveliest actresses and dancers he could find, and as they sat there sparkling in their jewels, they prepared the rest of the audience for a dazzling evening. Nowadays very few people bother to dress up for the theatre, but many of the most famous ballets were born into a world that expected and enjoyed glitter.

When the curtain rises, be ready for another world. All you need in order to understand what is going on, is the brief outline of the story in your programme, but you will enjoy the ballet much more if you know a little about its background. Your programme will tell you who wrote the music, who thought up the story, who designed the costumes and scenery, and who worked out the steps (the choreography). It may also tell you when the ballet was first performed and the names of some of the famous dancers who have appeared in it. This may not seem very important – why should you care about dancers you will never see, people who danced the parts before you were even born – but once you become interested in ballet, you will discover that you do want to find out about them. Every ballet, even a brand new one, builds on what has gone before. And when you know a little ballet history, you will begin to see how ballet has developed, why it follows certain rules, and how to understand its language.

It started about five hundred years ago as a kind of court entertainment. When the king had important guests, he liked to give a great feast at which his musicians and dancers performed. They would choose a story which could be made to flatter the king and his guests, and each course was accompanied by a new scene. The visitors loved the idea and took it back to their own courts, and soon every king of any importance entertained his guests in this way. Henry VIII was very fond of these masques, as they were called, and the French king Louis XIV was famous for the very extravagant entertainments put on at his court. He loved dancing himself, and we know of one ballet in which he appeared at the climax as the Sun. This was to be one of his favourite parts, and it helped to give him his famous title of 'the Sun King'. He expected his friends and courtiers to join in, but after a time he demanded such a high standard that it was necessary to call in professional dancers. They needed to be specially trained, and so Louis founded an academy where they could study.

As dancing was so closely associated with court life, the steps reflected the way the courtiers moved and behaved. They were expected to be graceful, to raise their hats with an elegant flourish, and to bow in a dignified way. Such movements became part of the dance steps taught at the academy, and these form the basis of the steps still used in ballet today. The steps are also still called by their French names, and these are used by dancers all over the world, making French the international language of ballet. Ballet for All, a touring company which is part of The Royal Ballet, does a programme called *Sun King, Swan Queen* which includes some examples of early dances. So if you want to get some idea of how Louis XIV danced, this is your chance.

Ballet has its origins in the sixteenth century, though in its early days it looked very different from what we see now. The first ballets were performed in royal palaces and told stories of gods and goddesses, needing words to help explain the story. Sometimes the audience was given a programme in which the plot was set out, or the words were sung, creating a kind of opera-ballet. But after a while, dancing-masters began to feel that it ought to be possible to tell a story without using words. In 1717, one of them, John Weaver, put on a ballet at London's Drury Lane in which the dancers used gestures to convey their meaning. It was not a great success, and not many people in England seemed very interested in ballet anyway, but it was a different matter in France.

Although the elaborate costumes of the day with their long heavy skirts were not ideal for ballet, the dance was beginning to free itself. It was helped by Jean Georges Noverre, a dancing-master who believed that dancing should be more than just a pretty display. He wanted to see it able to express ideas, and he wrote a book called *Letters on the Dance* which had a great effect on other teachers. The Royal Danish Ballet, which was founded in 1748, still performs a ballet that dates from this period. You might think it would have been forgotten by now, because in those days there was no way of making a record of the steps, but one generation of dancers has passed them on to the next, and thus the old ballet has been preserved.

At the beginning of the nineteenth century ballet, like all the arts, came under the spell of a romantic view of life. The Romantic Movement changed the way people thought about life. They began to look below the surface of things, and became interested in emotions and passions. As the Industrial Revolution took men away from the land and brought them into a world of machines and noise, dirt and smoke, there was a longing to escape. Attention turned, not surprisingly, to a world other than the real, unpleasant one. People became fascinated by dreams, ghosts, spirits, strange romantic characters and stories, and ballet was just the right setting for such illusions. The first great Romantic ballet, which is still being danced today, was *La Sylphide*, the story of a beautiful spirit who lives in a forest. The spirit was danced by Marie Taglioni, and she wore one of the most beautiful costumes ever devised. It was very plain and simple, just a white muslin dress with a long full skirt, but it was perfect for a sylph and has remained a favourite dress of dancers and audiences.

Dancing now found its wings as female dancers learnt how to rise on to the tips of their toes and dance *sur les pointes*. This seems to have happened for the first time in 1814, and it was the ideal movement for the spirits who began to float through ballets. Up to this time male dancers had been the more important figures, but suddenly they found themselves pushed into the background. Their chief function became to support and lift the ballerinas, and this sudden limiting of their role, when they had been famous for their leaps and the range of steps they could perform, was to have a very bad effect on ballet.

If you want to know what the dancers of this period looked like, you will find some lovely engravings of Marie Taglioni, Carlotta Grisi, and Fanny Elssler in the book *Ballet, An Illustrated History* by Mary Clarke and Clement Crisp. They all look very sylph-like in their filmy dresses, and it is easy to understand why audiences were so enchanted. They danced in ballets such as *La Sylphide*, *Napoli* (a Danish ballet in which a fisherman rescues his bride from the kingdom under the sea), and *Giselle* – ballets which you will have a chance of seeing as they are still performed by lots of companies.

The ballerina was now the star. As a result, male dancers became less accomplished, and ballet was no longer thought of as much of a career for a man. Things were different in Russia, but boys in the West were not encouraged to be dancers, and when The Royal Ballet first started in England, it was very short of men. This has changed now, partly thanks to the Russian dancer Rudolph Nureyev, who has shown how exciting good male dancing can be. The energy with which he bounds round the stage and leaps into the air has caught the public's fancy. Instead of looking cissy, he has brought out the strong, athletic qualities of male dancing.

By the end of the nineteenth century, ballet was in a poor state, except in Denmark and Russia, both of which had built up marvellous companies. It was still part of court life in Russia, but many of the nobles also had their own dancers, who entertained them at home. The dancers in the Imperial Ballet (the companies in Moscow and St Petersburg that belonged to the Emperor) were trained at special schools, and it was a great honour to be chosen to dance before the Emperor. Later on, we shall find out what it was like to go to one of these schools.

Huge sums of money were spent on staging ballets in Russia, and the finest teachers in the world were invited to St Petersburg to pass on the secrets of their skill. It was a Frenchman, Marius Petipa, who created many of the greatest successes, and you will hear more about him when we take a look at his most famous ballets – *The Sleeping Beauty*, *Swan Lake*, and *The Nutcracker*.

Petipa's ballets gave dancers a chance to show off their skill in dazzling solos, but dancing should have more to offer than this. One man who felt very strongly that the expression of feelings and ideas was more important than technical brilliance alone, was a young dancer called Michel Fokine. He disliked the way in which dancers cared only about their own parts rather than about the ballet as a whole, and he felt that the music, the scenery, the costumes, and the dance steps should be more closely connected to the subject of the ballet. Thus, if it happened to be about Greek gods and goddesses, for example, the dancers should wear the right costumes and try to copy the movements of the period. The painters Leon Bakst and Alexandre Benois, the dancer Vaslav Nijinsky and the composer Igor Stravinsky all shared his ideas, and with the help of Serge Diaghilev, they created ballets that were to have a lasting influence on dancers all over the world. Diaghilev was such an important person that he deserves a chapter all to himself, so you will be hearing a lot more about him in Chapter 4.

Audiences in Paris and London were thrilled by Diaghilev's Ballets Russes, when the company went on tour. It was the first time Russian dancers had performed outside Russia, and it revealed what an exciting form of entertainment ballet could be. Although the company danced some of the older ballets such as *Giselle*, the real impact was made by Fokine's ballets. The dancers, trained in the strict discipline of the Imperial schools, seemed capable of the most incredible steps, and the music and décor (the costumes and scenery) were exotic and colourful. The only other dancer who was later to make the public so aware of ballet as an exciting, moving experience was Anna Pavlova, and she too was trained at the same school and for a short time danced with Diaghilev's company.

Oddly enough, the Ballets Russes never danced in Russia, and when they finally broke away from Russia altogether, they found a home in Monte Carlo, on the French Riviera. There were always plenty of dancers who were eager to join such a marvellous company. When it was disbanded on Diaghilev's death in 1929, it had inspired dancers who were to take ballet to all parts of the world and, most important, to form companies in other countries. Thus George Balanchine went to New York, Serge Lifar to Paris, and Marie Rambert and Ninette de Valois to London.

Ballet in the West was also helped by the many dancers and teachers who left Russia after the Revolution and took refuge in Paris and London. They brought with them the methods used in the great Russian schools, and their pupils later became the new stars of the 1930s and 40s. The Diaghilev tradition was continued by the Ballet Russe de Monte Carlo, who put on ballets by two of Diaghilev's discoveries, George Balanchine and Leonide Massine. The company was also famous for its trio of 'Baby Ballerinas' – Riabouchinska, Baronova, and Toumanova. They were only in their early teens (Toumanova made her debut at eleven), and the press and public made a great fuss of them.

Since those days ballet has become much more popular, and many more countries have started their own national companies. We shall be looking at some of these later on, and also finding out how England's Royal Ballet, which started life as a handful of dancers helping out at the opera, became one of the top companies in the world. As you can see, ballet has survived and increased in popularity because it has been able to make the change from being an entertainment for kings to an entertainment for ordinary people.

Now that we've filled in some of the background, let's try and sort out just what a ballet is. So far we have talked about it in terms of dancing, but dancing is only one of its ingredients. A ballet also needs a theme or story, music, scenery and costumes, and the most successful ballets are those in which all these parts are just as important and just as good at carrying out their job. This doesn't often happen, but there are ballets (*Petrushka* is one) in which the right story finds the right music, the right artist paints the scenery and designs the costumes, and the right choreographer (the person who arranges the steps) works out the dances.

What is the right story? Well, it doesn't have to be about swan maidens or sylphs, or princes and princesses, though these do appear in some of the greatest ballets. The stories can be about all kinds of people, as you will soon see if you look at some of the recent programmes of The Royal Ballet. They include a ballet based on a game of chess (*Checkmate*), one about the composer Edward Elgar and his friends (*Enigma Variations*), one about an artist who falls in love with a gypsy (*The Two Pigeons*), and one about the dashing Captain Belaye of H.M.S. Hot Cross Bun (*Pineapple Poll*). So there is obviously no such thing as a typical ballet story. What these ballets do have in common, however, is that their stories have all been worked out so that they can be told in dancing. Ballets don't have to be about people in the past – the characters can be any age, the story can be sad or funny, or both, but they can't tell the kind of story that needs a lot of explaining. Thus the right story is one about situations that don't need words and can be expressed simply by the dancing.

But some ballets don't tell a story at all. They can be compared to a poem which tells you about a moment, a feeling or an experience, but doesn't have the same shape as a story. Such ballets may be about a mood, such as the feelings of a young girl after she has come back from her first dance (*Le Spectre de la Rose*), or about a group of people who happen to bump into each other in the park (*Les Rendezvous*) or go skating together (*Les Patineurs*). There are also abstract ballets where the interest lies in the shapes and patterns made by the dancers on the stage. If you are the sort of person who likes listening to music that pleases you just by the pattern of the notes, you may find that abstract ballets give you the same kind of pleasure.

Story-ballets are easier to enjoy when you first start going to the ballet, and they tend to be prettier to look at, as they often need fairly elaborate costumes and scenery. These can cost enormous amounts of money, whereas abstract ballets can often be staged much more cheaply with a plain backcloth as scenery, practice dress (the clothes worn for classes and rehearsals) for the dancers, and some clever lighting. Many people like such plainness and feel that it helps to direct attention to the dancing, but others feel that they enjoy a ballet far more if it is also colourful, exciting, splendid, enchanting or simply pretty to look at. You will get a chance to sample the various kinds of ballets, and probably very different kinds of décor, if you go to a triple bill (a programme made up of three short ballets). Another type of short ballet which sometimes appears on such programmes is the *divertissement*. This is a group of dances which are meant to show off the brilliance of the dancers. They are often part of ballets that are no longer performed in full, or they may be the highlight of a familiar ballet, such as the *Black Swan* which is one of the most famous dances from *Swan Lake*.

The kind of dancing we have been talking about so far, and will be in the rest of this book, is known as classical ballet. This means that it follows certain rules about the kind of steps used and the way in which the body and limbs are posed. These steps and poses are only possible after a lot of hard work and training, and they produce an ideal that is best described by such words as harmony, balance, grace and good line. But they are not the right words for modern dance, which prefers to have its feet firmly on the earth rather than flying through the air as in classical ballet. Its aims are so different that it really needs a book of its own to explain how it has developed and what it is trying to do. There are some fine modern dance companies, particularly in America where the great name is Martha Graham, and many new ballets, such as those now being done by the Ballet Rambert, are very influenced by the experiments of modern dance.

Apart from seeing as many ballets as possible, the other way to learn about ballet is to read about it. The more you know, the more you will work up an appetite for the ballets you want to see. Reading about past dancers and productions isn't nearly as dull as it sounds, because the past is never really dead. It affects the newest pupil starting his or her first term at ballet school and the newest spectator going to the ballet for the first time. They will both discover a lively world that makes demands on them and is full of echoes from the past mixed up with plans for the future. They are like someone going to the cinema and coming in half-way through the film. What follows is a chance to catch up on the first half of the story.

2·What makes a star?

Only a few of the hopefuls who train as dancers every year turn out to have the kind of magic that can fill a theatre anywhere in the world. Margot Fonteyn, Rudolf Nureyev and Natalia Makarova can attract audiences who may know very little about ballet, because they have some special quality – but what is it? Perhaps we shall find out if we take a look at some of the finer points and try to understand the qualities that make up great dancing.

First of all, how does a top dancer, or any kind of dancer, start? It takes many people a long time to find the right career, but time is one thing dancers don't have. They need to start their training when they are young, so that their bodies can be shaped to stand up to the special strains involved in dancing. Although their movements always look so easy and natural (this, after all, is part of the skill) many of the positions and movements involved in ballet – the ways in which dancers stand and turn their limbs – would be quite impossible for the ordinary, untrained adult.

Take the five positions of the feet. These are the basis of all steps in classical ballet, which begin and end in one of these positions. They involve turning the legs and feet out so that the toes point sideways instead of forwards, and this has to be learned and practised as early as possible. And if you still think the five positions look easy, try asking an adult to do them. They may just manage them at a pinch, but they won't look very comfortable or elegant!

Another movement that needs a lot of practice is dancing on tiptoe (or on *pointes*). Most people think of this as the one thing that distinguishes ballet from other types of dancing, though in fact ballet had existed for more than two hundred years before female dancers stood on tiptoe. The feet need a lot of strengthening and preparation for pointwork, so don't imagine that all a dancer needs is a pair of shoes with hardened toes to be able to flutter round as a swan or a sylph.

If you've ever had dancing lessons yourself, you will know that children start dancing for all sorts of reasons. Sometimes it's just because they like it, or it may be because their mothers are keen on the idea, or even for health reasons. Alicia Markova, the first outstanding British ballerina, was said to have had dancing lessons as a cure for flat feet – and you couldn't have a more unromantic reason than that! The traditional idea is that great dancers feel they are 'born to dance' – that they have an instinct that drives them to learn to dance, whatever the difficulties in their way. But is this true? Let's look at what some famous dancers have written about their childhood years and how they started to dance.

There are several accounts of Rudolph Nureyev's early life in Russia (by Alexander Bland and John Percival, both very good ballet critics), and according to these, when he was a very small boy he knew that 'the only thing I wanted was to dance'. His father was a soldier away at the war, and the Nureyev family was very poor. They lived in a small village in a remote part of the Soviet Union called the Bashkir Republic, and they were often short of food. It certainly wasn't the best place to try and learn something as fancy as dancing. When he was seven, Rudolf learned some of the local folk-songs at school, and he soon found that he enjoyed dancing and singing more than anything else.

He didn't, of course, know anything about ballet, but people who saw him dancing around used to say that he ought to go to Leningrad, where there was a marvellous school that would be ideal for him. But there was no money for luxuries like that, so Rudi just went on dancing and hoping that one day a mysterious stranger would turn up and give him the chance he so longed for.

Opera and ballet have always been very popular in Russia – and not only in the big cities like Moscow and Leningrad. All the republics have their own companies, and one day a ballet performance was announced at the Nureyevs' local theatre. His mother could only get one ticket, but all the family went along and somehow managed to squeeze in with the crowd. Rudi was thrilled by everything. He loved the theatre itself, with its velvet and gold decorations and the glittering crystal chandeliers. He felt that he had entered a fairy-tale world in which dreams came true, and the ballet itself was so wonderful that he knew he would have to become a dancer.

But there seemed to be no way of doing this. He lost interest in his schoolwork, and this angered his father, who had hoped that his son would become a doctor or an engineer. These were the kind of opportunities now open to poor people – the opportunities his father had fought for – and he was very disappointed that all his son cared about was dancing. What sort of a career was that?

Rudi managed to get lessons from an old lady who had once danced with Diaghilev's company, and she told him about the great dancers of the past, including the legendary Anna Pavlova. She said that Pavlova was so gifted and so well trained that her dancing seemed effortless and completely spontaneous, as though she were appearing for the first time and had dreamed up a new dance. Rudi made up his mind that one day he would dance like this too.

As he grew older, he had to hide from his family the fact that he was still having dancing lessons, but things improved when he got a chance to walk-on at the local opera house. Although all he had to do was walk across the stage dressed as a page or a beggar he was now earning money, and this pleased his parents. Despite his lack of proper training, the director of the Ufa Opera was impressed by his talent and keenness and offered him a regular job in the *corps de ballet* (the group of dancers who are not soloists and all dance together). But Nureyev was set on going to Leningrad, and even when he was offered the chance of a place at the Moscow Ballet School, he turned it down.

So finally he took the train to Leningrad and rushed to the Kirov Ballet School to apply for a scholarship. He had to show what he could do, and after the examiner had watched him jump and do the usual exercises, she came up to him and said: 'Young man, you'll either become a brilliant dancer – or a total failure. . . . And most likely you'll be a failure.'

It wasn't a very encouraging beginning, but what did it matter? He was awarded a scholarship, and at the age of seventeen – an age normally thought too old for a beginner – Nureyev entered the Kirov Ballet School and started proper training at last.

The way in which Anthony Dowell took up dancing was very different. His parents sent him to a stage-school in the first place because his sister went there, and it made life easier to have both children at the same school. The children learned acting, singing, tap-dancing and some ballet, and once he had appeared on the stage in a school performance, Anthony realised that he loved the theatre. He had a toy theatre of his own and liked designing sets and costumes for it but, unlike Nureyev, his heart was not particularly set on becoming a dancer.

He saw dancing as a way of getting on the stage, and when he went to the Royal Ballet School at the age of eight, he says he hated it. He wasn't a boarder at the school, as his family lived in London, and he longed to get back to his model theatre, which he found much more fun and more challenging than dancing. Dancing seemed easy, even rather boring, and it wasn't until he moved up to the senior school that he discovered how much there was to learn. Anthony Dowell is now thought by some critics to be the best classical male dancer The Royal Ballet has ever produced.

Being taken to see a ballet is often one way of finding out that you really want to dance. The great Russian dancer Anna Pavlova was taken to see *The Sleeping Beauty* as a Christmas treat. Her mother told her the story and said that she was going to visit fairyland. Afterwards, she asked Anna if she would like to learn to dance the waltz, which is one of the most inviting tunes Tchaikowsky ever wrote and is danced by the *corps de ballet*. 'I should rather dance the part of the Princess,' said the ambitious eight-year-old. 'One day I shall be the Princess and dance on the stage of this theatre.'

Pavlova was so determined to become a dancer, that she made her mother take her to the Imperial Ballet School. She was told to come back again when she was ten. Although it meant leaving home and going to live at the school, Pavlova didn't change her mind. She came back as soon as she was ten, passed the entrance exam, and to her great joy entered the School of the Imperial Ballet in St Petersburg.

Pavlova was to become the inspiration of a whole generation of girls who wanted to dance, but although Margot Fonteyn was taken to see her, she is honest enough to admit that she wasn't greatly impressed. Fonteyn started dancing lessons when she was only four. Dancing seemed a natural part of life, and although the sight of Pavlova didn't have any immediate effect, she tried harder with her dancing afterwards. Her mother had praised Pavlova, and she was determined that she would reach the same level of perfection.

Fonteyn had an unusual childhood – her father had a job abroad, and at one time the family lived in China. While there, her mother looked for the best teacher she could find, and Fonteyn had lessons from an elderly Russian lady who encouraged her to invent dances of her own, and then from another Russian who had danced at the Bolshoi Theatre in Moscow. When they returned to London, she had learned enough to impress Princess Serafine Astafieva. The Princess, who had been to the Imperial School at St Petersburg and danced in Diaghilev's company, was one of the many aristocrats who had left Russia at the time of the Revolution. She had opened a ballet school in London, and one of her great successes was little Alicia Markova (the child with flat feet), who had been chosen by Diaghilev when she was only fourteen. Fonteyn had a lesson with the Princess every day, and found that she made the most difficult movements seem a lot easier. The first time her partner lifted her up, she found it a very strange feeling – 'rather like being caught up in a tree by the shirt-tails'. The Princess told her to take a deep breath and hold on to it while she was being lifted, and also to keep her back very straight. The next time was much better – and lighter work for her partner, too.

Fonteyn would have been happy to continue with the Princess, but her mother had her eye on the future. She marched her off to the Sadler's Wells Theatre in Islington, where something very exciting was happening. As we shall see later on, it was here that British ballet was coming to life, and Fonteyn, who became a pupil of the Vic-Wells School, was to be the new company's first home-grown star.

In the next chapter we shall be taking a look at life at a ballet school, but for the moment let's go on trying to find out what makes a star. In the first place, looks are very important. The ideal shape for a ballet dancer is slim with a small head, a long neck and good proportions. Female dancers should not be too tall, as dancing on *pointes* will add a few inches to their height and they must not loom over their male partners! You might think that features wouldn't matter too much. After all, how many people in the audience can really see a dancer's face? But it is surprising how much you do see, how much an expressive face contributes to the interpretation of a part, and how hard it is to be moved by a dancer with an unsympathetic face. If you look at photographs of Margot Fonteyn in her great roles, you will be able to see the kind of soft, wistful, appealing expression that made her portrayal of young love so touching. You will find that it is often dancers' faces that attract you first, and if you don't like their faces, it is difficult to be fair about their dancing.

'Good proportions' means having a body and arms and legs that are all the right size in relation to each other. This is vital to a quality known as good line, which is often mentioned when critics praise dancers. Line can be difficult to appreciate until you have trained your eye to know what to look out for. A dancer arranges his or her head, body, arms and legs in such a way that they make a pleasing pattern in space. You can think of this pattern as an invisible circle drawn round a dancer. Whatever the arms and legs are doing, they always move within this invisible circle and touch its edge. It is easier to see the effect of good line in the pose called an arabesque. There are lots of different arabesques, but the main idea is that the dancer stands on one leg with the other stretched out behind, and has one arm out in front and one behind to form the longest line possible from the tips of the fingers to the tips of the toes. If the proportions are right, the result is beautiful, but if the limbs or the back are too long or too short, it doesn't look nearly as good. Line is also affected by turn-out – the way in which a dancer turns the feet and legs out at an angle to the body – and by the way in which the head, shoulders and arms are carried. You may not notice this at first, but when you are watching famous dancers, try to see whether there is anything special or different about their movements. Of course all dancers try to have good line, but some seem to have a natural gift for it – an instinct for making themselves into a lovely shape.

Another important quality is musicality. This doesn't mean that a dancer has any special musical knowledge, though most dancers study music and many of them learn to play an instrument. Musicality is the way in which a dancer responds to music and interprets it. If you are seeing a ballet that has been created by someone who has fitted the steps to the music perfectly, you should feel that the music and the dancing are absolutely together – that the dancing is, as it were, unfolding the music. When a dancer forges this link with the music – a link that is more than just keeping in time (though this is important, too) – then you are watching someone with real musicality.

Like all skill, musicality shouldn't look clever or difficult, and this is even more true of good footwork and the harmony between the ballerina and her partner. Audiences often clap when they see dancers do something that looks difficult, as when Nureyev goes whirling round the stage in his *Le Corsaire* solo, but they are not really paying him a compliment. Ballet is not about doing difficult steps, but about using steps to express such feelings as joy, sadness or energy. The audience should be involved in what is going on and should not be aware of how clever it is. Speed, precision, neat footwork and technical brilliance are all important, but if you find yourself thinking how clever a dancer is, then in a sense he or she has failed. When a ballerina is lifted up into the air or her partner catches her in some spectacular way, such as a fish dive, you shouldn't be wondering how much she weighs or what would happen if he dropped her. Ballerinas should look as light as thistledown, and although they may have spent hours if not days practising a movement, it should look easy, natural and as though they had just thought of it.

Dancers also need to be able to act, so that they can not only dance a part but round it out with feelings and emotion. Many ballets are about very dramatic situations, and a story such as *Romeo and Juliet*, which has been used for several ballets, needs a couple who are not only young and beautiful but can also spell out their tragedy to the audience like actors in Shakespeare's plays. Margot Fonteyn, for example, has always been able to make her audience share her feelings, especially when she played a girl in love. Lynn Seymour, who dances with The Royal Ballet, has a special talent for dramatic parts. In *Anastasia*, she played the youngest daughter of the Russian royal family, the only one who may not have been murdered in the Revolution. At the beginning, she is a happy schoolgirl, skipping round the stage, teasing the soldiers, and playing with her little brother; then we see her making her first appearance at court at a very grand ball; finally, she is a sad, bewildered figure who has suffered terribly. To dance a part like that you need to be more than simply a good dancer — though Lynn Seymour is certainly that, too.

One of the most exciting gifts of a male dancer is what is known as 'elevation'. This is the ability to do the kind of steps, such as an *entrechat*, that involve leaping and jumping. The Russian dancers have always been very good at this, and one of them, Nijinsky, became world-famous for the way in which he jumped through a window at the end of a short ballet called *Le Spectre de la Rose*. He played the spirit of a rose brought home by a young girl from her first dance, and he had to seem like a being from the spirit world, someone who could just float through space. People who saw his final leap were not only impressed by its height — and it doesn't really matter just how high he jumped — but by the way in which he seemed to hang in the air before he landed. Landing is just as important as jumping up, because if a dancer comes crashing down on to the stage, it completely destroys the idea that he is weightless and can fly. Nureyev is another Russian who is famous for his elevation. If you look at some of the photographs in Alexander Bland's book *The Nureyev Image*, you will see how often the camera has caught him with his feet way off the ground. The pictures also give you a good idea of what makes his dancing seem so exciting.

Even if a dancer has pleasing features, good proportions, beautiful line, musicality, dramatic gifts and good technique, he or she will still not be a star without one more quality. There are different words for it: personality, charm, sex-appeal, magnetism or charisma. They all add up to the same thing, and it is something that takes a dancer out of the *corps de ballet* and puts him or her

27

alone in the centre of the stage. It is the kind of magic that sells tickets, fills theatres, and brings dancers wave after wave of clapping and cheers at the end of a performance. Sometimes ballet audiences overdo this, but they certainly don't do it for everyone, and it does show the effect a great dancer has.

Personality can make up for other defects. Sometimes you will hear people say that a famous dancer lacks musicality or has a far from perfect technique, and you wonder how they came to be a star if it is true. The answer is always personality – the gift of being able to stand out from the rest, so that once on stage all eyes are upon you. If you see Nureyev dance, you will find that the audience is waiting for him to come on and watches him even when more important things are happening. Even when he was much younger, he was able to outshine other dancers, often by doing the most simple things. Whereas many male dancers seem to wonder whether they really are or ought to be a prince, Nureyev is confident that he is one. He wears his costume with a swagger, and knows that he can make the audience believe in him. It is his ability to attract this kind of attention that has made him a superstar, and ballet without such stars, however good the other dancers are, would seem very flat. They bring an excitement that keys up the audience and the rest of the company, and often set a standard neither can forget.

3·Learning to dance

The great ballet schools such as the Kirov in Russia, the Royal Danish Ballet School and the Royal Ballet School in England all leave their own special mark on pupils. We have seen how several of the most famous students got into ballet school, so now let's take a look at the kind of training they received.

Probably the best known ballet school in the world, and certainly the oldest, is the Kirov School in Leningrad. It was founded in 1735 by a tsarina (the wife of the Russian emperor, or tsar), and it was originally called the Imperial Ballet School because of its close connections with the Imperial family and the Court. The Tsar and Tsarina liked to visit the school, and the pupils sometimes took part in special performances given in the delightful little pink and white theatre in the Hermitage Palace. Anna Pavlova is said to have burst into tears when Tsar Alexander kissed another little girl whose dancing had pleased him, and Nijinsky was given a gold watch by the Tsar.

The school building is a grand eighteenth-century palace which stands in a beautiful street. It once had a very appropriate name, Theatre Street, but has now been renamed Rossi Street. Children from all over the Soviet Union come to be auditioned for a place, and they need to be very strong and healthy because the training is very hard. Anna Pavlova, Vaslav Nijinsky and Tamara Karsavina, three of the school's greatest pupils, have described what life was like when they were there at the beginning of this century. In those days the pupils were regarded as being in the service of the Emperor, and the boys wore peaked caps with a silver

29

badge in the shape of the Imperial eagle. After two years as day-boys, which meant that they lived at home, they became boarders and were given the complete, very smart uniform. This was like the uniform worn by the boys at the Cadet School, and had a high velvet collar embroidered with a silver lyre, the special badge of the school. The everyday uniform was black, the holidays one dark blue, and the summer one was made of grey linen. The boys also wore long military overcoats with silver buttons, and leather boots. The girls wore thick blue dresses that had tight, low-cut tops and long, full skirts, white fichus (scarves), black or white aprons, white stockings and black shoes. Even at the time, it was an old-fashioned style of dress, and it emphasised the way in which the pupils were cut off from the rest of the world. Boys and girls kept to different parts of the school and were forbidden to speak to each other, but sometimes they danced together and would slip each other notes.

Each day had a strict timetable. The students got up at 7.30, washed, had breakfast, and were then marched off for a walk. There were dancing lessons until lunch-time, a rest after lunch, and then classes in French, maths, the history of ballet, music, mime and make-up. After supper there were games or fencing, but not the usual school sports, as these would have developed the wrong muscles. Sometimes the students played small parts in the operas and ballets put on at the nearby Maryinsky Theatre. They were driven to the theatre in special coaches, known jokingly as Noah's Arks, and had their own dressing-room apart from the other dancers. It was a life centred round ballet in every way. When Tamara Karsavina had to go to the dentist, he said to her, 'Have patience; a future prima ballerina must have pretty teeth.' No wonder that the students devoted all their energies to one goal – becoming members of the Maryinsky Theatre company.

Of course many things had changed by the time Rudolf Nureyev became a student at the school. The Tsar and his court had long been swept away, St Petersburg had changed its name to Leningrad, and the Imperial School and the Maryinsky Theatre were now called the Kirov – all changes that reflected the different form of government that had taken over after the Revolution of 1917. But the basic routine of the ballet school had not changed all that much.

Nureyev shared a dormitory with nineteen other students and ate all his meals in the large dining-room. He spent most of the day studying, with lessons on art and literature, two hours of classical dancing, lunch, classes on the history of ballet and music, and then two hours of character dancing. He also had to study science, geography and fencing. After supper, Nureyev would watch the Kirov company rehearsing or go to a performance. On one occasion, when he rushed off without asking permission, he came back to find that his bed had been taken away. He had to spend the night on the floor, and got a stern lecture from the Director next day.

As he didn't join the school until he was seventeen, it was difficult for him to accept the rigid discipline. He insisted on being in the eighth grade, and this annoyed the other students, who didn't like the idea of dancing with someone who was still a beginner. But the teaching was so good, and Nureyev was such a natural dancer, that in his second year he won the right to dance the leading roles. And when he graduated, he was offered a place in both the Bolshoi and the Kirov companies.

Ideally, all ballet companies need their own school so that they can train dancers in the particular style of the company. Ninette de Valois, the Founder and first Director of The Royal Ballet, had the advantage of dancing with some of the most famous Russian dancers and realised how much they owed to the superb training of the schools attached to the Bolshoi and Kirov companies. She wanted to start a British ballet company – a very adventurous idea in the 1920s – but she saw that she would have to begin with a British ballet school. So in 1926 she opened The Academy of Choreographic Art – an impressive name for what was really a very small dancing school. We shall see later on how she made her dancers into a company. The important point here is that when they were offered the chance to become part of the newly-opened Sadler's Wells theatre, the school went with them.

At first the school only taught dancing, but as the company grew larger and more successful, de Valois began to make plans. She knew that dancers also needed a good general education, which would make them better dancers and also fit them for other jobs if they had to give up dancing. Her ideas were shared by Arnold Haskell – a critic whose books had helped to interest many people in ballet. When a full-time school was opened in 1947, he became the director and headmaster. But it was only really suitable for children who lived in London, so the next goal was a boarding-school that could take pupils from all over the country. The answer turned up in the shape of White Lodge – a handsome house in Richmond Park that was designed as a hunting lodge for George I and is surrounded by parkland where you can still see deer. It took over the junior school in 1955, and the next year the whole school was officially renamed the Royal Ballet School.

There are about 125 pupils at White Lodge, most of them boarders, and they have got there by passing an audition. Children take the exam at the age of eleven, and it involves some simple exercises of the kind taught at all dancing schools. The examiners aren't at all impressed by clever dancing. They are much more interested in how tall a child is and in the shape of the feet and the proportions of arms and legs, because they have learned from experience what kind of body stands up best to the demands of dancing. As we have seen, good line is one of the qualities of a great dancer, and although training can help to develop this, it also depends on being the right shape in the first place. As you would guess, feet are very important because they have to take a lot of strain, and some types of feet don't wear well and could cause trouble later on. Of course personality, intelligence, temperament and musicality matter too, and there is always an element of chance, as ugly ducklings sometimes turn into swans.

In many ways White Lodge is much like any other school. The pupils study for C.S.E. or G.C.E. exams and learn the usual subjects such as English, maths and biology, as well as music and history of ballet. At first dancing is limited to one or two periods a day plus a class. Class is something that dancers take the whole of their dancing lives, and it involves routines that are much the same the world over. All dancers need strength, control, and stamina or staying power. They need to be able to depend on their muscles to meet the demands made on them. These qualities are gradually built up by a programme of exercises that must be carried out every day, both by the newest student and by the most experienced dancer. They help to warm up the muscles (which are then kept warm by those very unromantic woollen leg-warmers you often see in practice photographs) and make them flexible. The first exercises are done with the help of a barre, a wooden rail on to which the dancer holds lightly while bending and stretching, and the walls of the practice studio are lined with mirrors so that the dancers can keep checking their positions. The exercises are followed by groups of steps, or *enchaînements*, and some teachers are world famous for their ability to invent groupings that dancers find particularly helpful.

However spontaneous ballet may look – as though the dancer had been inspired by feeling or the music and burst into dance – it is in fact all very carefully planned. Each dance is made up of a series of steps, which are strung together like the words in a sentence. All the basic classical steps are taught at White Lodge, as well as character dancing, folk dancing, Morris dancing and Benesh notation. This last item is a system for recording on paper the steps of a ballet, so that it doesn't just depend on dancers' memories. It was invented by Joan and Rudolph Benesh, and uses the five lines of a music stave. These represent a dancer's head, shoulders, waist, knees, and the floor, and lines and dots mark the position of the feet and hands and show the changes in their position. The stave can be written under a line of music, so that it is clear how the notes and steps match up. Pupils sometimes go to see ballets at Covent Garden and occasionally take part, as in Nureyev's production of *The Nutcracker*, but such appearances are rare. White Lodge does not see itself as a forcing house for baby ballerinas.

At the end of each year there are tests to see whether it is still a good idea for a boy or girl to continue with a career in ballet. There is a high dropout rate, sometimes because pupils are growing too tall, or because they don't feel as enthusiastic as they did at eleven. Even some of those who stay until sixteen and then go on to the Upper School may change their minds, finding that dancing is too demanding and takes up too much time, or that they are good at something else and prefer to go to university. It is a career with a great many drawbacks, and only very determined dancers are likely to survive.

The students at the Upper School come not only from White Lodge but from teachers and schools all over the world. Many of them come to train as teachers, and some want to take back to their own countries the special style of dancing associated with The Royal Ballet. The Upper School is in a most unromantic part of London, with a motorway to London Airport rushing past, but perhaps this is the right setting for a career that involves very hard work and plenty of competition. Students learn classical ballet, *pas de deux* (dancing with a partner), character dances, drama, Spanish dancing and stage make-up, and once a year they put on a performance at Covent Garden. The Royal Ballet Company also uses the school for classes and rehearsals, and a few students may be invited to join the company or its touring section, which is now called the Sadler's Wells Royal Ballet. Other students will join companies such as the London Festival Ballet, The Scottish Ballet, or perhaps one of the many foreign companies that welcome dancers trained at such a fine school.

This doesn't mean instant fame, however, because dancers who join a company at seventeen or eighteen usually find themselves at the bottom of the ladder. Although in the past some dancers played leading roles when they were very young – Beryl Grey, for example, danced *Swan Lake* on her fifteenth birthday – this happened in special circumstances, such as wartime, when there was a shortage of dancers and new talent was needed as quickly as possible. Nowadays few dancers under twenty-one get the chance to dance leading roles. It usually takes at least three or four years to reach the top rank of principal dancer, and this only happens to the best. The others may dance on as members of the *corps de ballet* or become solo artists, playing increasingly important parts but never the lead.

Many principal dancers are not equally good at all kinds of parts, just as some actors are better at comedy or tragedy. A dancer's best roles often depend on his or her physique and personality. The great classical ballets such as *The Sleeping Beauty* and *Swan Lake* call for dancers with a strong technique, beautiful line, and the kind of personality that shines through sheer skill and can make a great impression in parts that are not strongly defined. Thus the ballerina playing Princess Aurora in *The Sleeping Beauty* doesn't tell you much about the character of the Princess, but her dancing can be youthful, sparkling, and full of happiness. The *demi-caractère* dancer, on the other hand, shines more in parts that are sharply drawn and need qualities such as warmth, charm, a sense of humour and acting ability. The greatest dancers, such as Fonteyn, can play a wide range of parts, but a fine classical dancer may not be so happy with light-hearted or dramatic parts, and the dancer who is marvellous at these may not be at his or her best in strictly classical roles. Then there is the character dancer, usually male, who is brilliant at unusual or comic parts. One of the finest of these is Alexander Grant, who created the part of Alain, the simple-minded youth in *La Fille Mal Gardée* who has no idea how to woo a girl and is much more worried about his umbrella. Another character part in this ballet is the Widow Simone, who does a superb clog dance to a very catchy tune. Two of the funniest parts are the Ugly Sisters in *Cinderella*. These were first danced by Robert Helpmann and Frederick Ashton, who plainly enjoyed themselves very much. Character dancers need to be nimble and acrobatic and to have a gift for clowning and mime. Many story-ballets also have parts for older dancers, and The Royal Ballet is lucky that it can afford people such as Gerd Larsen and Leslie Edwards, who make splendid parents or elderly courtiers.

But sadly few companies are able or want to keep on dancers once they are past their prime, and this happens all too soon. Although Fonteyn has been dancing for more than forty years, she is an exception. Most ballerinas are at their best between thirty and thirty-five, and usually retire before they are forty, while the men have even shorter careers. Many ex-dancers become teachers, open dancing schools, or help to run a ballet company. Beryl Grey is now the Artistic Director of the London Festival Ballet, and Celia Franca and Peggy van Praagh have built up companies in Canada and Australia. Some dancers discover a talent for choreography (working out the steps for a ballet), but this is a very rare gift; others take up acting in the theatre or films.

It may seem hard that so much training is needed for a career that doesn't last very long, but all dancers go into it with their eyes open. They accept the uncertainty right from the beginning, when they know that they may grow too tall, or not make the grade, or be injured and unable to dance for weeks, if ever again. Although they are now well paid, at least in the top companies, they were just as keen in the days when dancers earned only a few pounds a week. Nowadays many people want a safe, steady job which offers security, but dancers choose a way of life that can never be like this. They buy the glamour you see on stage at the price of a long training, constant practice, self-discipline, and the kind of dedication that turns a job into a way of life.

4 · Diaghilev and friends

This chapter is about famous names of the past – about a group of dancers, choreographers, composers and artists who were brought together by one man and with his help changed the history of ballet. The man was Serge Diaghilev, and he was born in Russia in 1872. He came from a home that was full of music, but although he would have liked to become a musician himself, he realised that he was not quite good enough. Instead, he was sent to St Petersburg to study law, and there he met a cousin who introduced him to his friends. They were all very interested in the arts and two of them, Léon Bakst and Alexandre Benois, were painters. In no time at all Diaghilev had forgotten about his legal studies and become caught up in the exciting world of his new friends. He discovered that he liked looking at paintings, that he was a good judge of them, and that he knew talent when he saw it. This ability was to prove one of his greatest gifts. All through his life he was to recognise what was new and good, and was to have the courage and the money to back his beliefs.

He was made the editor of a new art magazine, and soon became involved with the Imperial Theatres, the Bolshoi and the Maryinsky, where he had the chance to see operas and ballets. In 1906 he decided to try an experiment: he would stage an exhibition of Russian art in Paris. It was the first time many of the paintings had been seen outside Russia, and it was a huge success. It was obvious that people in the West enjoyed Russian art, so perhaps they would also like Russian music. Diaghilev organised a series of concerts at the Paris Opéra, and he arranged for some of

37

the composers, such as Rachmaninov and Rimsky-Korsakov, to go to Paris to conduct their own works. The audiences loved the singer Féodor Chaliapine, who had a wonderfully rich bass voice, and this gave Diaghilev the idea of staging a whole opera. He chose *Boris Godounov*, hired the chorus of the Bolshoi Theatre and the best singers available, with of course Chaliapine in the part of Boris, and ordered magnificent new costumes and sets. The result was a triumph, and the problem was what to do next. Then Diaghilev had a brilliant idea. He would give Paris audiences something else new – their first glimpse of Russian ballet.

He chose the ideal moment for his venture, because the Russian ballet was going through a period of change thanks to Michel Fokine. Fokine had been trained as a dancer at the Imperial Ballet School in St Petersburg, and had joined the company as a teacher and soloist. He was a fine dancer, but he was not at all satisfied with the way in which the ballets were staged. Instead of concentrating on the story, and making sure that the dancing, the music, the sets and the costumes were in keeping with it, everything revolved round the ballerina and was designed to show off her skill. Many of the dances had nothing to do with story, the ballerina always danced on tiptoe and wore a tutu (a short skirt made of frills of net), and the action was often interrupted by applause for the solos. This infuriated Fokine, who never allowed dancers in any of his ballets to accept applause until the end. Many audiences today will clap a spectacular piece of dancing, but artistically Fokine was quite right – a burst of noise can so easily break the spell cast by an enchanted lake or a beautiful pattern, or spoil the flow of the music.

Fokine was also a gifted painter, and he spent a lot of time in museums and art galleries, studying pictures and sculpture and trying to absorb the mood and style of the stories of the past. When he began to create his own ballets, he took great care that the elements were right for the story. Thus the music was not chosen because it was pretty or dramatic, but because it suited the story, and the dancers' costumes were in the style of the period in which the story took place. His greatest innovation (or new idea) was to make the steps themselves tell the story, so that there was no need for the long passages of mime that had been used in the old ballets. In Fokine's ballets everything that needed to be said was said by dancing, not actions, and in this way he revolutionised ballet.

Diaghilev's interest in ballet had been roused by his great friend, the painter Benois. It was really Benois' idea to stage ballet in Paris, and he spoke enthusiastically about the many good young dancers and the exciting new ballets by Fokine. He had designed the set and costumes for Fokine's latest success, *Le Pavillon d'Armide* (1907), and he persuaded Diaghilev that it was just the thing for Paris. Together they also agreed to take two other Fokine ballets, a series of dances to music by Chopin which was given the new title of *Les Sylphides*, and a ballet about the Egyptian queen, Cleopatra. Diaghilev then set about hiring the best dancers he could find in the Moscow and St Petersburg companies. These included Anna Pavlova, Tamara Karsavina, Adolf Bolm, and a promising newcomer called Vaslav Nijinsky.

Nijinsky had finished his training at the Imperial School of Ballet in 1907, and instead of having to start in the *corps de ballet*, he was chosen as a soloist and given the honour of partnering one of the most famous ballerinas. As a student he danced in Fokine's first ballet, and Fokine was quick to recognise his extraordinary talent. Although Nijinsky was to become the greatest dancer in the world, he was disappointing to meet off-stage. He was short and thickset, his legs bulged with muscles, and he was not at all handsome but had a shy, quiet expression and strange slanting eyes. He was not very exciting to watch at rehearsals either, because he moved in a rather mechanical way, but when he put on his costume, he became a different person. Benois said that when Nijinsky looked in the mirror, he changed into the person he saw reflected there. The need to be disguised affected his dancing. Although he danced the Prince in *Giselle* and *Swan Lake* very well, he seemed more inspired when he became a character such as the mischievous Harlequin in *Carnaval* or the sad, tormented puppet, Petrushka.

On the opening night in Paris, Nijinsky played the Favourite Slave in *Le Pavillon d'Armide*. He wore a white, yellow and silver jacket trimmed with silk, lace and ermine tails, and a white silk turban with an ostrich feather. His solo had lots of high jumps, and the audience soon realised that he was something special. Then hordes of slave girls, wild tribesmen and oriental warriors spun round the stage in the savage Polovtsian Dances from the opera *Prince Igor*. The thrilling evening ended with a suite of dances, a hotchpotch that included the striking Blue Bird *pas de deux*, danced by Karsavina and Nijinsky. The critics were full of praise, the dancers were the toast of Paris, and audiences were just as delighted by the other ballets. They were particularly impressed by the strong, athletic male dancers, who were as important as the exquisite ballerinas.

Of course the dancers had to come back the next year, 1910, and this time they were invited to dance on the huge stage of the Opéra. They brought two new ballets by Fokine, *Schéhérazade* and *The Firebird*. The story of *The Firebird* was a mixture of Russian fairy-tales, and the startling music was by Diaghilev's latest discovery, Igor Stravinsky. Some of the dancers found his strange new rhythms difficult to follow, but Fokine thought the music was wonderful. In one of his finest dances, the Prince tried to catch the firebird as she fluttered round a darkened stage lit only by a golden spotlight. Then twelve Enchanted Princesses appeared and danced with golden apples from a magic tree. The ballet achieved something completely new: the ideas of the composer, the choreographer, and the designer fitted together perfectly.

At the end of the season Diaghilev went off for his usual holiday in Venice. When he returned to St Petersburg, he told his friends that he had decided to form a permanent ballet company of his own. He persuaded Fokine and Karsavina to sign contracts, and when Nijinsky lost his place in the Maryinsky company, he too was free to join Diaghilev. An assortment of dancers were recruited for the *corps de ballet*, and the great Italian teacher Cecchetti was hired to give them lessons every day. Serge Grigoriev became the *régisseur* (or general manager) of the company, and many years later he wrote a useful book about his experiences. Diaghilev was now launched on a definite pattern: he was always looking for new talent and commissioning new ballets. In twenty years he was to produce more than fifty, some of which are still being performed today.

The highlights of 1911 were two new ballets by Fokine – *Petrushka* (the story of a poor puppet who falls hopelessly in love) and *Le Spectre de la Rose*, which was to give Nijinsky his most famous part. He wore a costume covered in pink rose petals that always seemed to be falling to pieces. So many new petals had to be sewn on that questions were asked. Where were they disappearing to? It was discovered that Nijinsky's dresser was besieged by admirers wanting souvenirs, and that he had been snipping off the petals and selling them. There was such a demand, that he was said to have bought a house with the proceeds! Later that year, when Diaghilev took the company to London, Nijinsky scored another triumph. The British public fell in love with the Russians, though some of them were a little shocked by the *Prince Igor* dances. Bakst's brilliant coloured scenery and costumes made such an impact that purple and red suddenly became favourite colours.

By now Nijinsky was no longer satisfied with being a dancer. He wanted to create ballets as well, and Diaghilev was delighted to give him the chance. Nijinsky had very definite ideas. Just as Fokine had broken away from the past, so Nijinsky wanted to break away from Fokine's style and discover one of his own that would reflect modern life. First of all he threw out the familiar classical steps. Instead, he made his dancers use jerky movements and turn their toes in. In his first ballet, *L'Après-midi d'un faune* (1912), the poses were inspired by one of those ancient Greek reliefs that show the figures sideways rather than facing the onlooker. As none of Nijinsky's ballets have survived, it is difficult to judge what the effect was like, but they were not popular with the audience. At the first night of *Le Sacre du Printemps* (*The Rite of Spring*) in 1913, they howled, whistled, and shouted insults. One young lady was so angry with the man in the next box, who was hissing, that she slapped his face. Her escort and the man exchanged names and the next day fought a duel. We don't know what happened, but let's hope it wasn't serious!

Stravinsky's music was just as strange as the dances. The rhythms were difficult to follow and the orchestra had to cope with weird new sounds. There were only seven performances, and apart from the music, now recognised as brilliant, all that remains are a few sketches of the dancers, the reviews of the critics, and the memories of some of those who took part. *Le Sacre* was ahead of its time – the first of the kind of experiments that were to lead to the free-for-all of modern dance.

Nijinsky's friendship with Diaghilev came to a sudden end when he fell in love with a rich, very attractive girl who had been allowed to take lessons with the company. When Diaghilev heard of their marriage, he was furious, and he soon found an excuse to dismiss Nijinsky. Nijinsky then tried to form his own company, but he was a dancer, not a businessman, and he needed the kind of help only Diaghilev could provide. As there was now a war on in Europe, Diaghilev wanted to take his company to America, but the American public insisted on seeing Nijinsky. They had to make up their quarrel, but they were no longer close friends. Nijinsky was not well. Sometimes he behaved very strangely. In the autumn of 1917, at the end of a South American tour, he danced in public for the last time. He was twenty-nine, and he planned to go on dancing, to create more ballets, and to start a ballet school. But it was not to be. His mind was disturbed, and soon he was seriously mentally ill. He never recovered, and although he lived until 1950, as a dancer he had died more than thirty years before. Although his career was so short, it spanned some of the most exciting years of ballet. Richard Buckle has written a fascinating, very long book about Nijinsky's life, which will tell you a lot more about his circle of friends.

Fokine, who had hated Nijinsky's ballet experiments, had also parted from Diaghilev, but he too was persuaded to return. Ballet was moving on from his ideas to even newer ones, but *Le Coq d'Or* (1914) proved how much audiences still loved his work. They also enjoyed the lively music by Rimsky-Korsakov and the bold sets and costumes in brilliant reds and yellows. The magical golden cockerel of the title was only a stage prop, but when the ballet was revived in 1937, Fokine turned it into a dazzling role for a ballerina, who has to dance on her pointes all the time to show that she is a fairy-tale creature. This is a ballet you can still see, as the London Festival Ballet did a new production of it in 1976. Fokine did one more ballet for Diaghilev and then returned to Russia. Later he went to live in the United States, where he died in 1942. He went on creating ballets, but his best work had been for

Diaghilev. Now, as Diaghilev saw, ballet wanted something quite different.

This turned out to be a young dancer called Leonide Massine, whom Diaghilev had met in Moscow. Massine had been thinking of becoming an actor instead, but Diaghilev's offer was so tempting that he couldn't refuse it. While the company were away in America, Diaghilev improved Massine's dancing and tried to turn him into a choreographer. Convinced of his talent, he took him to museums and art galleries to increase his knowledge and give him confidence. The result was *The Good-Humoured Ladies* (1917), an amusing story taken from an old play and danced to tinkling harpsichord music.

Diaghilev also liked to try out new designers, and he invited Pablo Picasso to do the sets and costumes for *Parade* (1917), an odd little ballet about circus folk. The two circus managers were given the most fantastic costumes that made them look like cubist paintings come to life. The dances were arranged by Massine, who played a Chinese conjuror and did tricks with an egg. There was also a Little American Girl who pretended to be acting in a silent movie, a frisky pantomime horse that sat down very elegantly, and two acrobats. They all put on a lively show to try to attract the public, but the fun ends on a sad note because no one wants to see the show. When the London Festival Ballet revived *Parade* in 1976, they copied Picasso's original designs, so you have a chance to see how strange and effective they were.

During the 1914–18 War the company found life difficult. There was not enough money to pay the dancers, the only country to welcome them was Spain, and they often danced in very primitive conditions. But in 1919, they were offered a proper season at the Alhambra theatre in London. Massine's new ballet, *La Boutique Fantasque* – about a toyshop in which the toys come to life – was very popular. He followed this with his masterpiece, *The Three-Cornered Hat*, which had a Spanish theme and reflected his recent visit to Spain. He played the main part and gave a splendid display of Spanish dancing in the *farruca*, which he had been specially taught by a young Spaniard. Picasso was the designer, and he painted a dramatic front-curtain showing a group of Spaniards at a bullfight. These act-drops, as they were called, were used in a number of ballets, and the most famous ones, such as those by Picasso, were later sold for vast sums of money.

Now it was Massine's turn to fall out of favour with Diaghilev. They had begun to quarrel as Massine became more experienced as a choreographer and wanted to have his own way. One day Diaghilev sent a·message to say that he had no further use for him and that he was free to leave the company at once. Massine was to return some years later, and in the 1930s he was artistic director of the Ballet Russe de Monte Carlo. He created several ballets for them including *Le Beau Danube* (1924), danced to the famous Blue Danube waltz by Johann Strauss. In 1947 he helped the Sadler's Wells Ballet stage some of his ballets at Covent Garden, and he repeated his wonderful performance as the Miller in *The Three-Cornered Hat*. You may have seen him in an early British ballet film, *The Red Shoes*, in which he played the shoemaker who made the fateful shoes that wouldn't stop dancing. His ballets are occasionally revived today (the London Festival Ballet have a couple in their current repertoire). The best ones are distinguished by lively, dashing, character parts.

Meanwhile Diaghilev, faced with the problem of finding a new ballet for his 1921 London season, and with no choreographer of his own, decided to update an old ballet. He chose one with music by Tchaikowsky, rechristened it *The Sleeping Princess* (it is better known as *The Sleeping Beauty*), sent for his old friend Bakst and gave him the daunting job of designing five new sets and over a hundred costumes. He engaged three Russian ballerinas to take turns at dancing the Princess Aurora, and spent much of his time directing the production himself. It was the kind of ballet he had loved as a child, and he wanted audiences in the West to enjoy a full-length classical ballet. But it was not a success, and lost a lot of money. The British public had a different picture of Russian ballet, and were not yet ready to admire such a display of pure dancing. Since then, audiences have come to realise what a splendid, theatrical ballet it is, and how well it shows off the talents of the whole company. But poor Diaghilev was ahead of his time. He could not even stage the ballet in Paris, as he had hoped, because the backer kept the costumes and scenery in part payment for all the money he had lost.

Diaghilev's search for a new choreographer was now rewarded. Nijinsky's sister, Bronislava Nijinska, had arranged some new dances for *The Sleeping Princess*, and it was clear that she had a gift for it. She created several ballets for Diaghilev including *Les Noces* (1923), a moving portrait of a Russian peasant wedding, and *Les Biches* (1924), a series of light-hearted flirtations among a group of young people in the 1920s. Both have been danced since by other companies. Frederick Ashton is a great admirer of her work and persuaded The Royal Ballet to revive these two favourites.

Diaghilev had now found the company a permanent home at Monte Carlo, and they danced there every winter. Talented new dancers continued to arrive. These included Serge Lifar, Alexandra Danilova, and Anton Dolin and Alicia Markova, who were to do so much to promote the idea that the English could be groomed into star dancers – providing they had Russian names to help them! Alicia Markova, whose real name was Alice Marks, was only fourteen when Diaghilev engaged her, but before long she was dancing solo parts. Another important recruit was a young man from the Imperial Ballet School in St Petersburg. Georges Balanchivadze (now George Balanchine) was to be Diaghilev's last choreographic discovery. One of his early ballets, *Apollo* (1928), which shows the birth of the god Apollo and the way he teaches the three Muses their skills, is still a favourite of Nureyev and The Royal Ballet. His very dramatic ballet *The Prodigal Son* (1929) is currently danced by the Sadler's Wells Royal Ballet and needs a strong male dancer in the title role. When the Diaghilev company came to an end, Balanchine travelled round and finally settled in the United States. In 1948 he became the artistic director of a new company, the New York City Ballet, and created many works for them. One of his most popular is *Serenade* (1934), which has no story but will seem familiar if you know Tchaikowsky's *Serenade for Strings*, with its beautiful, irresistible waltz.

By now Diaghilev had lost some of his enthusiasm for ballet. He was not well, his spirits were low, and he seemed more interested in his collection of rare books. At the end of the 1929 season he went off to Venice, which had always been one of his favourite cities. There he died. He had always dreaded travelling by sea, because a fortune-teller had once told him that he would die on water. If you know Venice, a city that seems to float in the sea, you will see how right the fortune-teller was.

Although his death meant the end of his company, Diaghilev's influence was certainly not at an end. The ballets he had helped to create, the dancers he had made and the choreographers he had encouraged all went on. The words 'danced with Diaghilev' were a passport for dancers all over the world. They passed on their memories in books, through their teaching, and in new product-ions of his ballets. Today there is still great interest in this period, when the ballet world was young and brimming with talent. In 1954 Richard Buckle staged a famous exhibition to commemorate the twenty-fifth anniversary of Diaghilev's death, and there has often been talk of making a film about him. So if you're interested in ballet, it is useful to know who Diaghilev was and what he did.

Before we find out what was happening to ballet in England, there is one more important Russian name you should know about – Anna Pavlova. This is the right place to include her, be-cause in the early days of her career Pavlova too danced with Diaghilev's company.

Pavlova studied at the Imperial Ballet School in St Petersburg, and was a frail child who had to be fattened up with cod-liver oil. But there was nothing frail about her determination to become a great dancer. At first she danced with the Imperial Ballet and went on tour with them. She made a great impression on audiences who knew nothing about ballet, and she realised that she had the power to make people happy – to help them to escape from re-ality for a short time. She was invited to dance with Diaghilev's company on their first visit to Paris, but did not enjoy sharing the limelight with Karsavina and Nijinsky. She was not in sympathy with many of Diaghilev's ideas, and found Stravinsky's music, for example, very ugly. She preferred to appear on the music-halls with her own group of devoted dancers. Although she was only one item in a programme that included all sorts of acts, like a modern variety show, she was well paid and was able to bring ballet to the sort of audiences who would never have gone to an opera house.

Fokine greatly admired her soft, romantic dancing, and it was he who created her most famous solo, *The Dying Swan*. She was to dance this all over the world, and it was the one piece that every audience wanted to see. She seemed to be transformed into the dying bird, fluttering its wings and shuddering as it sank to the ground. In her other solos – *The Dragonfly*, *The Butterflies*, *Californian Poppy* – she expressed some magical quality that made the simple little dances unique. The desire to reach new audiences drove her round the world, from South America to Australia and the East. Dancing classes boomed, and at least one small boy, Frederick Ashton, who saw her dance in Peru, had the course of his life changed by the experience. People responded to Pavlova's personality as much as to her dancing, but fellow dancers and critics also praised her extraordinary talent. Today all that is left is memories, photographs, and some rather poor silent films. But if you read what has been written about her dancing, you will get a glimpse of her greatness, and learn something about the qualities a dancer of real genius possesses.

5 · Ballet in England

If you liked ballet in the 1920s – and in those days not many people did – you thought of it as something Russian. But a few years later, ballet fans were trekking out to Islington and Notting Hill Gate, outside London's theatreland, to see two small groups of dancers and young choreographers prepared to work very hard for very little money, and led and inspired by two very determined ladies, Ninette de Valois and Marie Rambert.

Ninette de Valois was a child prodigy who went on dancing when she grew up. She danced in pantomime and at Covent Garden, and in 1923 she joined Diaghilev's Ballets Russes. She was soon made a soloist, but her heart was not set on becoming a ballerina. She wanted to start a company that would bring together English dancers, choreographers, artists and musicians, and create the kind of favourable artistic atmosphere that Diaghilev had provided. And she realised that to develop a truly English style of dancing, she would need a constant supply of well-trained dancers.

The best way to achieve this seemed to be to start a dancing school, but although hers had the very imposing name of The Academy of Choreographic Art, it was only a small affair. The next thing her handful of dancers needed was the chance to appear in public, so de Valois went to see Lilian Baylis. Lilian Baylis was another determined woman with splendid dreams. She wanted to start a National Theatre, and had got as far as staging operas and plays by Shakespeare at the Old Vic – a theatre in a very unsmart part of London. She liked Ninette de Valois and

1 *(below)* The greatest ballerina of all time, the Russian Anna Pavlova. This picture shows her in the costume she wore to dance *The Dying Swan*

2 *(right)* The great Russian dancer Vaslav Nijinsky in the costume for his most famous role as the spirit of the rose in the ballet *Le Spectre de la Rose*

3 *(right)* The expressive face of the young Margot Fonteyn, seen here in the mad scene from *Giselle*

4 *(below)* Rudolf Nureyev doing one of his spectacular leaps – a good example of the excitement of male dancing

5 *(far right)* Anthony Dowell and Natalia Makarova in practice costume. Woollen legwarmers keep the dancer's muscles warm and flexible

6 (above) The Royal Ballet in an early production of Les Sylphides, the Romantic ballet to music by Chopin

7 (below) Act 1 of The Royal Ballet's production of Anastasia, showing Lynn Seymour as the young Anastasia

8 Natalia Makarova in a beautiful classical pose. She ran away from the Kirov Ballet while they were visiting London in 1970 and later joined the American Ballet Theater, but often makes guest performances in Britain

9 *(left)* One of ballet's panto-mime dames – the witty clog dance from *La Fille Mal Gardée*, created for The Royal Ballet by Frederick Ashton in 1960

10 *(below)* Michael Coleman as Jeremy Fisher in the delightful film of *The Tales of Beatrix Potter*, performed by The Royal Ballet

11 *(overleaf)* A dramatic example of modern ballet – Joseph Scoglio and Julia Blaikie in Ballet Rambert's production of *Pierrot Lunaire*, to music by Schoenberg

admired her spirit. There was no money to spare, but she agreed to pay £1 a week for dancing lessons for the actors and singers, £2 if the play or opera needed a short dance, and £3 for any extra dances. It wasn't much (though not quite as little as it sounds today), but it gave de Valois a steady income and, more important, a shop-window for her dancers.

One of Miss Baylis's dreams was of opening another theatre. She had her eye on a derelict building in Islington, and gradually she raised the money to rebuild Sadler's Wells. (It is called after a Mr Sadler, who lived there in the seventeenth century, and the wells in his country garden are still there today, under the stalls and the stage.) Meanwhile de Valois' little band of dancers (at first, six girls and a teacher) were not only appearing in the operas, but putting together dances of their own. One of these was put on one night before the opera and was such a success that Miss Baylis realised that audiences might enjoy a whole evening of ballet.

This idea was encouraged by the Camargo Society, which was called after a famous eighteenth-century ballerina and formed in 1930 to advance the cause of English ballet. Its members were people who were prepared to give money so that new ballets could be staged three or four times a year. The dancers and choreographers came from the de Valois and Rambert schools, leading artists and musicians designed sets and wrote special music, and although the society lasted only three years, it produced sixteen new ballets. The most important was *Job* (1931), which was inspired by the superb drawings the artist-poet William Blake had done for the Bible story many years before. The dances were arranged by de Valois, and the ballet later became a great success when it was staged at Sadler's Wells. Another favourite, which has often been revived, was Frederick Ashton's *Façade* (1931), a lighthearted joke that makes fun of some of the dances of the 1920s.

The other founder of English ballet, Marie Rambert, was also a member of Diaghilev's company. Born in Poland, she took up dancing in Paris and studied Dalcroze eurhythmics (a method of understanding music by learning to put movements to it). Diaghilev heard of her skill in this, and asked her to help his dancers work out the difficult rhythms of the music Igor Stravinsky had written for *Le Sacre du Printemps*. At first she was not interested in classical ballet, but later she came to London, took lessons with the great Italian teacher Cecchetti, and was completely won over. She decided to open a dancing school, and one of her first pupils was Frederick Ashton, a young man who had seen Pavlova dance and found ballet far more his line than a career in the City. She soon realised that he had a gift for arranging dances, and his first ballet was so good that she and her students were asked to dance it in a London revue. The costumes were designed by Rambert's friend, Sophie Fedorovitch. This was the start of one of the great artistic partnerships of English ballet, as Fedorovitch always provided Ashton with just the right settings and costumes, as you can still see.

In 1927 Rambert's husband (the playwright Ashley Dukes) bought an old church hall in Notting Hill Gate and converted it into a studio and tiny theatre. They called it the Mercury, and thus the Ballet Rambert (as it was later known) became the first English company to have its own school and theatre. The students were soon good enough to put on a season at a London theatre, and Karsavina was sufficiently impressed by their talent to dance with them and teach them some of the ballets she had learned with Diaghilev. Cheered by their success, Rambert and her husband decided to start a supporters' club, and in 1931 the Mercury became the home of the Ballet Club.

That same year the Sadler's Wells theatre opened, and de Valois handed over her school as a training ground for the new Vic-Wells Ballet. The name reflected the job of the company, which was to put on opera-ballets at both theatres. The dancers would rehearse at the Wells and then dash across by bus to the Vic, which was on the other side of London. It was a tough life. There was no room to practise, dressing-rooms were crowded, the mice had a passion for the glue on pointe shoes, and there was very little money. There was no Arts Council in those days; the company had to pay for itself. The first full evening of ballet was helped off the ground by Anton Dolin, an English dancer who had made a great name for himself while dancing with Diaghilev's company. Its success led to ballet once a fortnight, and Alicia Markova joined Dolin as the great attraction. They performed some of the ballets created for the Camargo Society, but de Valois soon realised that they would have to tackle the classics, too. This was made possible by Markova, who was a guest dancer for these first vital years and danced in *Swan Lake*, *Giselle* and *The Nutcracker*. She was partnered by Dolin and by a young Australian, Robert Helpmann, who joined the school and was soon playing leading roles. When she first met him, de Valois is supposed to have said, 'Something can be done with that face.' She had spotted an acting talent and sense of theatre that were to prove just as important as his dancing.

Over at the Mercury, Rambert's gift for attracting and developing talent was paying dividends. The Ballet Club ensured a full house, and although some of the dancers had to take jobs in musicals and revues, they always managed to get back for the Sunday and Thursday performances. Markova was seen here too, and was paid 10/6d (about 50p) to appear, which just about covered her taxi fare home. Although the stage was tiny, the décor simple, the costumes often improvised and the 'orchestra' seldom more than a piano, the ballets themselves were works of art. The atmosphere was stimulating, and Frederick Ashton, Antony Tudor (another late starter who worked as an accountant and then rushed across London for lessons), and Andrée Howard (also a fine dancer) created exciting, dramatic, poetical ballets. We can only read about most of them now, as they are impossible to revive, but it is worth reading Mary Clarke's *Dancers of Mercury*, which gives a lively picture of the dancers and ballets of these early days.

Although they were separate companies, there were many links between the Rambert and de Valois dancers and choreographers. Some left the Mercury for the Wells, and in 1935 Frederick Ashton, who had created his first important ballet, the sparkling *Les Rendezvous* (1933), as the guest of the Vic-Wells Ballet, was invited to join them on a permanent basis. Today The Royal Ballet calls him its 'founder choreographer', and his career is largely the story of how the company has developed. His ballets (and he has composed nearly a hundred) have given dancers wonderful opportunities, sent them in new directions, formed great partnerships, and given English dancing its distinctive qualities. He is a master of story ballets, as you can see in the current productions of the lighthearted, amusing *La Fille Mal Gardée* and the tender, thoughtful *The Two Pigeons* (1961), in which a young artist chases after a beguiling gipsy girl only to find that he is much better off with his first love. He is also a master of the plotless ballet, from the magical *Symphonic Variations* (1946), with its moving simplicity into which you can read whatever you like, to *Monotones* (1965/6), in which two groups of mysterious but confident figures carry out cool, ordered movements that match the strange music perfectly. Try to see this if you can, and see if it makes you think of calmness, order, grace, precision – moving sculpture.

Other Ashton ballets that you may have the chance to see include *The Dream* (1964), *Enigma Variations* (1968) and *A Month in the Country* (1976). *The Dream* is danced to the well-known music by Mendelssohn (including that old war-horse the Wedding March). It presents the essence of Shakespeare's *A Midsummer Night's Dream*, with Oberon quarrelling with Titania and making her fall in love with Bottom the weaver, wearing his ridiculous ass's head, and Puck darting round and getting the unhappy lovers even more mixed up. The dancing is featherweight and emphasises that this is a story about weightless spirits. It is made up of darting, soaring, spinning movements that are just right for the impish music.

A Month in the Country is based on a play by the Russian writer Turgenev. The heroine, Natalia, is a spoilt woman who is bored with life in the country and, not surprisingly, falls in love with the handsome student who arrives to tutor her son. He is obviously much more fun than her dull husband, and he pursues not only the mistress of the house but her young ward and the maid, too. Boredom is not easy to express in ballet terms, but Ashton gives the characters brilliant solos that make their feelings as clear as in the words of the play. He is always marvellous at portraying love. Here he shows its different aspects as the student flirts with the maid, has a tender duet with the young girl, and dances passionately with Natalia.

Ashton has also composed some full-length ballets, such as *Cinderella* (1948) and *Ondine* (1958), in which he has adapted the conventions of the great Russian classical ballets to the theatre of today. His strengths as a choreographer are his ability to tell a story in a dramatic way and weave all the characters together, his sense of humour, which has produced some very funny character parts, and his poetical understanding of love, which makes the *pas de deux* the highlight of his ballets and which has been so radiantly interpreted by Margot Fonteyn.

Margot Fonteyn was the first, and is still the greatest, dancer produced by The Royal Ballet. Like Ashton, her career has spanned its growth and coming of age. She was singled out as a soloist before she was sixteen, and when Markova left the company, many people thought that they would never survive without a star. But Ninette de Valois had faith in her young dancers, and pushed Fonteyn in at the deep end. At sixteen she was dancing Odette in *Swan Lake*, and at seventeen, very much against her will, she was playing Giselle. In her autobiography she says that she felt she would never be able to do the steps, that her face was like a pudding, and that she was being pushed into the great classical ballets against her will. On the opening night de Valois' telegram read: 'And some have greatness thrust upon them.' It is a quotation from Shakespeare which begins, 'Some are born great, some achieve greatness ...' This seems even more appropriate now.

Of course the critics praised Fonteyn, and if she was then too young to understand the full tragedy of what happened to Giselle, her performance was touching because it was genuinely youthful. Many of the greatest parts can only be danced by ballerinas when they are much older than Juliet or Giselle are meant to be, but Fonteyn has the gift of always seeming just the right age.

She has portrayed the gaiety and tenderness of young love and the sadness and heartbreak of parting with unforgettable feeling. She is too old to play such parts now, but what you have missed are not displays of brilliant dancing (other members of the company have equalled and bettered her technique) but an ability to communicate feelings that is a far more rare and precious talent. Fonteyn's unique personality inspired and matched the moods Ashton translated into steps, and together they have developed what is thought of as the English style, with its soft, poetical qualities. Her main partners have been Robert Helpmann, Michael Somes and Rudolf Nureyev. Her special understanding

53

with Nureyev brought an extra magic to their dancing, and Ashton recognised this in his ballet *Marguerite and Armand* (1963), a love story that will probably never be danced by anyone else. Fonteyn's success showed that the Sadler's Wells Ballet could produce a world-class dancer and give her the scope and support that a really great ballerina needs.

Other triumphs of the company's early days were the ballets of Ninette de Valois (one of which, *Checkmate* [1937], is still danced by the Sadler's Wells Royal Ballet) and the brilliant musical direction of Constant Lambert, who came up with inspired suggestions for music for new ballets, as well as fine dancers such as Harold Turner, Robert Helpmann, Pamela May, June Brae, Michael Somes, Moira Shearer and Beryl Grey, and some enchanting sets and costumes by artists such as Rex Whistler, Oliver Messel, and Leslie Hurry. During the Second World War the company moved to a smaller theatre. Most of the male dancers were in the Forces, and yet the show went on and a new, wider audience discovered ballet. Robert Helpmann was often the only male dancer around, and he turned choreographer too, producing the dramatic ballets *Hamlet* (1942) and *Miracle in the Gorbals* (1944). Covent Garden, which had been used as a dance hall during the war, was reopened, and the Sadler's Wells Ballet was presented with a much more splendid home. They staged a grand opening in 1946 with a lavish new production of *The Sleeping Beauty*, and felt confident enough to start a second company, which was known as the Sadler's Wells Theatre Ballet.

The Ballet Rambert was not so lucky, though it had built up a fine repertoire, including two ballets that you can see today – Antony Tudor's *Dark Elegies* and Andrée Howard's *La Fête Etrange*. *Dark Elegies* (1937) describes the grief of a group of parents after disaster has struck their village and killed their children. Tudor uses very simple steps, and has a remarkable gift for showing people's inner feelings in his ballets. His masterpiece, *Pillar of Fire* (1942), is about the jealousy between sisters competing for the same man. It was created for the American Ballet Theater, and since then Tudor has worked mainly in America.

Several of Andrée Howard's ballets took their stories from novels, and she was particularly attracted to fantastic, poetical subjects. Recent productions of *La Fête Etrange* (1940) have used the original beautiful backdrop designed by Sophie Fedorovitch, which shows the park of a country house deep in snow. The pale, wintry scene sets the mood of the ballet, which is a haunting story of misunderstandings and thwarted love.

Although her dancers often left to join other companies or start new ventures, Marie Rambert was always able to find promising newcomers. Money was a serious problem, but she carried on boldly, and in 1946 put on a new production of *Giselle* that recaptured much of the original charm of the old ballet. There was strong competition from the Sadler's Wells companies and the newly formed Festival Ballet, but they could not repeat the very special achievement of the Ballet Rambert. It was a small company with limited resources, but the limitations and, above all, Marie Rambert herself, proved artistically very stimulating. Gradually, however, the company found that it couldn't afford to go on staging full length ballets or touring with a large company and an orchestra, so in 1966 it was reorganised and streamlined. It was slimmed down to seventeen soloists, there was no *corps de ballet*, and it was decided to concentrate on modern ballets suitable for a small company.

One or two ballets from the old repertoire are still performed, but the accent is now on modern dance. Much of the re-shaping work was done by Norman Morrice, a very promising choreographer who studied with George Balanchine and Martha Graham in New York. The American Glen Tetley, an important name in modern ballet, has created several ballets for the company, and one of its biggest successes has been his *Pierrot Lunaire* (1962), which starred the Rambert's latest discovery, Christopher Bruce. Bruce started as a dancer, went over to choreography, and has now contributed eleven ballets including the charming *Girl with Straw Hat* (1976), which was inspired by a photograph of Marie Rambert as a little girl with a large hat and created to celebrate the company's fiftieth anniversary. Two special programmes you should try to see, especially if you want to sample modern dance, are *Take a Running Jump*, which traces the development of dance through the ages and ends with a performance of a Christopher Bruce ballet, and *Bertram Batell's*

Sideshow (1970), which has a danced weather forecast, a hunt in the jungle, and some stunning tumblers.

Once the Sadler's Wells Ballet had settled down at Covent Garden, it soon established itself as a top company. It paid a triumphant visit to the United States, where tough New York audiences were bowled over by *The Sleeping Beauty*, and its success was officially recognised in 1956, when the two companies were renamed The Royal Ballet. In the thirty odd years since the war, the company has danced many of the great classical ballets as well as twentieth-century classics by Fokine, Massine, Nijinska, Balanchine and Tudor. There have also been superb ballets by Ashton and by two new choreographers, John Cranko and Kenneth MacMillan.

Cranko had already staged some ballets in South Africa before he came to England and joined the second company at Sadler's Wells. His most popular ballets have proved to be the light-hearted *Pineapple Poll* (1951), a dance version of a Gilbert and Sullivan opera, and *The Lady and the Fool* (1954), a romantic little tale of two clowns and a beautiful lady with the moral that love is more important than riches. In 1961 he was offered the job of running the Stuttgart Ballet Company, and soon made it internationally famous. The leading dancers became stars, and he created some wonderful parts for the dramatic ballerina Marcia Haydée. Cranko composed some fine plotless ballets, but also enjoyed telling a good story, and did it very well. More than most choreographers, his ballets make you aware of the shape of the music by the way in which the steps seem to match and unfold the notes. Sadly, he was killed in an air-crash in 1973.

Cranko's colleague Kenneth MacMillan studied at the Royal Ballet School and became a fine classical dancer with the companies at Sadler's Wells and Covent Garden. Friends at Sadler's Wells persuaded him to try his hand at choreography, and the dances he arranged for their experimental group were a great success. His first major ballet, *Danses Concertantes* (1955), was full of clever ideas, and he went on to develop a gift for portraying strong inner feelings. Some of his finest works are about passion, frustration and loneliness. He has been inspired by the Canadian dancer Lynn Seymour, who is very sympathetic to his ideas and marvellous at interpreting his heroines, and he has also worked a lot with the designer Nicholas Georgiadis. Ballets you might specially enjoy are his version of *Romeo and Juliet* (1965), which uses the very dramatic music by Prokofiev, *Anastasia* (1971), which presents a beautiful, often moving picture of the doomed Russian royal family, and *Elite Syncopations* (1974), a series of fun dances to the catchy ragtime music of Scott Joplin. MacMillan was Director of The Royal Ballet from 1970 to 1977, when he resigned to become their principal choreographer. The new Director is Norman Morrice, who made such a success of the reorganisation of the Ballet Rambert.

The Royal Ballet is one of the greatest companies in the world. For most of the year it dances at Covent Garden, and has as principals such fine dancers as Lesley Collier, Anthony Dowell, Wayne Eagling, Desmond Kelly, Monica Mason, Merle Park, Georgina Parkinson, Jennifer Penney, Lynn Seymour, Antoinette Sibley, Wayne Sleep, and David Wall (you can find out more about them in Chapter 9). The company also attracts superb guest artists, such as the Russians Mikhail Baryshnikov, Rudolf Nureyev and Natalia Makarova, and the stars of the Stuttgart Ballet, Richard Cragun, Marcia Haydée and Egon Madsen.

The Royal Ballet isn't only for people who live in London. The Sadler's Wells company dances at theatres as far apart as Bournemouth, Birmingham, Leeds, Newcastle and Aberdeen, and the Ballet for All group, which aims to introduce ballet to people who have never seen it or who want to learn more about it, is able to use small stages and so visits some very remote places. Later on we shall be looking at some of the other companies that have sprung up in Britain, and telling you more about the ballets to look out for when a company comes your way.

6 · How a ballet is made

Some dances look so natural and spontaneous that you might think the dancers were doing whatever steps came into their heads at that moment. The music is joyful, the occasion a happy one – perhaps someone has just fallen in love – and the dance expresses just the way you feel when you're happy. But the steps themselves, though not the amount of expression a dancer puts into them, have all been carefully worked out beforehand. They are as fixed as the lines of a play, and just as actors aren't allowed to change the words, so dancers must do the same steps at every performance. Every dancer on the stage depends on this – just think how untidy the *corps de ballet* would look if some of the dancers were doing their own thing instead of all moving as one!

So if ballets have to be carefully planned, who decides in the first place what steps to use and explains them to the dancers? This is the job of the choreographer, or composer of the ballet, and because a ballet also needs a story, music, and sets and costumes, he has to work together with a lot of other people.

A ballet begins with an idea or a story. It may come from a book or an old fairy-tale, or it may be suggested by a few lines of poetry, a painting or a piece of music. The one essential thing is that it must be the kind of idea or story that lends itself to dancing. Thus it mustn't be too complicated, the action must take place through movements, and the movements must be bold enough to make their message clear to the whole theatre, right down (or up) to the back row of the gallery. George Balanchine, the great

American choreographer, once said that there are no sisters-in-law in ballet. And if you think about trying to explain such a relationship without using words, you will see what he means. Sisters-in-law just can't be done!

The story or idea then has to be developed into a scenario. This sets out in detail how the story is to be told. It divides it into scenes and acts, if it is to be a long ballet, and shapes it so that it is dramatically interesting, with plenty of things happening and a good climax. The scenario may be worked out by the choreographer, the composer of the music, the designer, a writer or poet, or perhaps a dancer, and it should provide a firm framework for the ballet. The best ballets are always those with a strong plot or basic idea, and the most beautiful music and costumes and the most skilful dancing can never save a story that isn't right in ballet terms.

Choreographers work out the steps in different ways. Marius Petipa, the maker of some of the greatest Russian ballets, used to start his work at home. He had little figures like chess pieces that he used to represent the dancers, and he would arrange these on the table to form various patterns and groupings. When he found one that pleased him, he wrote it down in his notebook. At rehearsals he would listen to the music and work out the dance in his head. Then he would send for the dancer and explain what he had in mind. The dancer would try out the steps, and Petipa would correct or change them as they went along. Finally he would ask to see the whole dance. In those days much of the action was explained by gestures, and when Petipa mimed these scenes he was quite carried away. The dancers were spellbound by his artistry and would clap loudly when he had finished.

But not many people work like this. Frederick Ashton goes to rehearsals with a clear idea of the story, the characters, and the kind of dances he wants. He likes to work out the steps with the dancers, and finds that some will suit certain dancers better than others. On a good day he may get a whole sequence sorted out but, as he says, you can't rely on inspiration turning up at ten o'clock in the morning, and it may take as long as a month to get a *pas de deux* just right. Most ballets are composed with particular dancers in mind, and many choreographers find one dancer who inspires

59

them. Thus many of Ashton's ballets were written for Margot Fonteyn, and Kenneth MacMillan finds Lynn Seymour's dramatic ability ideal for his ballets. She says about working with him, 'You come into the rehearsal as a kind of empty sponge,' and she feels able and ready to soak up his ideas. Sometimes a dancer may feel that the choreographer is asking too much of him or her. Then he must either make the steps easier or, as Ashton has done with Fonteyn, persuade her that she has the ability to do what seems impossible. Choreographers also have to cope with the problem of dancers' busy lives. This can mean that instead of starting at the beginning of a ballet, they have to work on whatever part suits the dancers who are free.

The music is often the main reason why certain ballets have survived. Tchaikowsky's *Swan Lake*, *The Sleeping Beauty* and *The Nutcracker* are popular partly because their music is so irresistible. It calls out to be danced and, unlike a lot of ballet music, never melts into the background to become just a pleasing noise. The other great composer who wrote special ballet music was Igor Stravinsky. He was one of Diaghilev's friends, and he challenged the idea that ballet music had to be light and tuneful with obvious rhythms. His music is often harsh and full of strange, even ugly sounds, but if you see *Petrushka*, you will realise how well it describes the inner feelings of the characters. Diaghilev had a genius for discovering new composers, and he commissioned music not only from Stravinsky but also from Debussy, Ravel, Manuel de Falla, Poulenc and Erik Satie. And the music they wrote for him, which sounded so advanced at the time, is often played in concert halls today.

Ballets have always made great use of existing music, and if you like music, you will recognise some of the tunes that turn up. Chopin's piano music has become so linked with ballet through *Les Sylphides*, that it is almost impossible to hear the famous Prelude without seeing dancers in filmy white dresses. Although it may seem wrong to have piano pieces played by an orchestra, the music is such an integral part of this ballet that it doesn't seem a mistake. Much of Chopin's music is in the form of dances such as waltzes and mazurkas, which are an open invitation to choreographers. The American Jerome Robbins, who arranged the

dances for the musical *West Side Story*, has produced two delightful Chopin-inspired ballets. *The Concert* (1956) shows a group
of people listening to a concert and the effects (some of them very
funny) that the music has on them. In *Dances at a Gathering*
(1969), five girls and five boys act out a series of relationships,
some funny and some sad. They wear plain costumes and there is
no scenery, so this is very much a ballet for people who enjoy
pure dancing – and Chopin.

Symphonies, concertos, pop music and tunes from Gilbert and
Sullivan and Verdi operas have all been used as ballet music. It can
be difficult to use music that is very well known, because the audience will already have given it their own meaning, and many
people who love Elgar's music, for example, must have wondered
whether they would enjoy his *Enigma Variations* as a ballet. But
Ashton used it to show how much his friends meant to the composer, gave a face and a form to the friends that Elgar was
portraying, and so produced a ballet that was in keeping with the
spirit of the music.

One ballet score that has had a great attraction for choreographers is the music that Prokofiev wrote about Romeo and
Juliet. The story of Shakespeare's unlucky lovers has always been
a favourite, and there were several ballets about it before the
Russian one was staged in 1940. In this version, Juliet was danced
by Galina Ulanova, the great star of the Russian ballet in the years
after the Revolution. Her performance was filmed and is still
shown in the West sometimes. The same music has also been used
by Frederick Ashton, John Cranko and Kenneth MacMillan, who
have all produced their own versions of the story and emphasised
different aspects of it. This is a tribute not only to the very dramatic story, with its quarrels, duels and unhappy love, but also to
Prokofiev's music, which is bold, striking, and immediately gives
the right feeling of doom. There are some good recordings of it
(and of all the Tchaikowsky ballets), and it is a good idea to get to
know some ballet music, particularly the kind that can stand on
its own feet as superb music.

As you will see from your ballet programme, music sometimes
needs to be specially arranged for a ballet, as in the case of *A
Month in the Country*, which used some early, almost unknown

pieces by Chopin. The arrangement is often done by the conductor, and one of the most famous ballet conductors was Constant Lambert, who was with the Sadler's Wells company from its early days up until after the war. He wrote some music himself, and was an expert at finding and arranging unusual music that was just right for dancing, as you can hear for yourself if you go to *Les Rendezvous* or *Les Patineurs*. The conductor of ballet must not only be a first-class musician, but must also understand the steps and know how to regulate the music to suit different dancers. They rely on him to set the pace, and they would soon be lost if he let the orchestra race ahead or play too slowly.

When it comes to the décor, the choreographer usually chooses the designer and they often form a partnership that inspires them both. Some of the top designers whose work you are likely to see include Nadine Baylis, Nicholas Georgiadis, Barry Kay, Osbert Lancaster, Leslie Hurry and Julia Trevelyan Oman. Some people today do not agree with the old idea that the scenery and costumes are at least as important as the music, and many modern ballets are danced in practice dress or something very near to it. This is a matter of taste and also, I suspect, expense. Staging a ballet costs a fortune these days. The 1975 *Sleeping Beauty* cost £55,000, and even a short ballet can be as much as £10,000. This is why you often hear that the ballet is short of money in spite of full houses and huge grants from the Arts Council and other organisations, who pay the bills that used to be met by kings and princes.

Although it is obviously ridiculous to spend too much on staging, it is wrong to say that it is unimportant. The American choreographer Paul Taylor once defined ballet as 'food for the eyes', and once you have seen one or two with enchanting sets and costumes, I think you will agree that they are more than just decoration. At their best, they can interpret the mood of the story as much as the music and the dancing.

The designer has to work with the workshop that builds the sets and with the wardrobe – that army of people who make and look after the costumes. He must remember that however elaborate they look, the costumes must be as light as possible, and whatever their period style, they must be easy to dance in. They have to stand up to very hard wear, and very unromantic conditions such as being drenched in sweat, and it is the wardrobe who mend the tears and see that the swans and sylphs don't come on looking bedraggled.

The first stage-call is the moment when all the different pieces of a ballet are fitted together. The dancers, who have probably been rehearsing to a piano, now get a chance to hear the full score and find out if they can manage their costumes. The stage staff have to sort out the scene changes, the lighting expert plots his course, and there may be special effects to try out, such as a flash of lightning or a puff of smoke. It is perhaps worst for the choreographer. Now his ballet is made, and the critics and the public will decide whether it will be seen a few times and then vanish, or whether it will become part of the regular repertoire. On the title-page of the Covent Garden programme you can read the number of performances that have been given so far of the ballet you are about to see. A recent one read, 'The 574th performance at the Royal Opera House by The Royal Ballet of *Swan Lake*.' That's the kind of record a choreographer dreams of!

7· Some popular ballets

You've enjoyed your first visit to the ballet and are longing to go again, but how do you decide what to see? Much depends on where you live, on which companies are available, and on the ballets being performed in their current season, but sooner or later you will probably have a chance to see all the ballets described in this chapter. Although many companies start with the idea of doing something new, audiences seem to prefer the old favourites, and both the London Festival Ballet and The Scottish Ballet soon found that they needed the classics to help pay for their more adventurous programmes. You may find as you grow older that you prefer modern dance, or ballets that seem more in touch with life today, or the kind of vast shows staged by Maurice Béjart and his Ballet of the 20th Century, which are a mixture of song, dance, speech, music and acrobatics, but it's a good idea to try and see the classics at least once.

The great classical ballets, some of which are more than a hundred years old, tell their stories in steps and movements that were invented in the early days of ballet. Even the costumes follow certain rules, and the heroine usually wears either a Romantic tutu – a beautiful, plain net skirt that falls well below the knee – or a classical tutu – a very short skirt made of frills of net. Although some aspects of the ballets may strike you as old-fashioned and not at all like real life, they have enchanted generations of ballet-goers, and it is worth trying to see why. They have certainly not survived because of their choreography, much of which has been forgotten and rearranged, but either because of their music, because their stories still appeal to the imagination, or because in many cases they offer dancers, especially ballerinas, an irresistible challenge. At some stage in her career every ballerina longs to dance in *Giselle*, *Swan Lake* and *The Sleeping Beauty*. Such ballets not only make the highest demands on a dancer, but give her a chance to take her place alongside Pavlova, Karsavina, Ulanova and Fonteyn. You may not be lucky enough to see such great dancers, but you may see someone at the beginning of what turns out to be a wonderful career. Years later you will be able to say that you saw X long before they were famous – and of course realised that they were something special. I remember noticing Anthony Dowell back in 1962, when he first joined The Royal Ballet. He attracted attention even in a small part, so see how good you are at star-spotting.

It's useful to know something about a ballet before seeing it. Knowing the story won't spoil the surprise, but will help you to sort out the characters and understand just what is going on. The oldest ballet still being performed is *La Sylphide*. It is still danced by the Royal Danish Ballet, who staged the first performance in 1836, and it has been revived by The Scottish Ballet, which is most appropriate as the story takes place in Scotland.

The sylph, or spirit, of the title appears one day in the home of a young Scotsman, James. She is an enchanting, rather mischievous spirit, and she flirts with James, who immediately falls in love with her. But he already has a girlfriend and is about to marry her, and he is furious when an old woman tells the young couple that they will never get married. James drives the old woman out of the house, and naturally enough she vows to get her own back on him.

Although James loves his girlfriend, Effie, he can't resist the charms of the sylph, who comes back again to tease him. When she flits off into the forest with the ring that was meant for Effie, James rushes after her. His friends go to look for him, but it is the old woman, who is really a witch, who finds him. She gives him a magic scarf and tells him that it will help him to catch the sylph. But when he slips it round the sylph's shoulders at the end of their dance together, instead of becoming his for ever, she droops and dies. A troupe of sylphs carry her body away, and at the same moment James sees a bridal procession passing by. Effie, persuaded by the witch that James no longer loves her, has married someone else.

The first version of the ballet, dating from 1832, has not survived, but it was in this version that the choreographer's daughter, Marie Taglioni, first wore the simple white dress that has become symbolic of Romantic ballet. Although in many Romantic ballets the male dancer was pushed into the background and not expected to do more than support and lift the ballerina, this is not true of *La Sylphide*. When the Danish choreographer August Bournonville rearranged the ballet, he gave James plenty of dancing and some fine solos which have attracted the attention of Nureyev.

Of course the Romantics, who loved stories about sylphs and spirits, were bound to enjoy *La Sylphide*, especially as it has an unhappy ending that illustrates their belief that love always ends in death. Perhaps it will seem moonshine to you, but it is worth trying to see the spirits in these early ballets as representing feelings and conflicts that trouble people in every age. Thus the nice girl that James is going to marry stands for the reality of everyday life, while the sylph is an ageless ideal of beauty that beckons James away from his responsibilities. Or as a modern James might see it, the sylph offers freedom and escape, whereas his girlfriend means settling down and accepting practical duties such as earning a living. If you think about it, you will see that falling in love can still cause this kind of conflict.

An even more popular Romantic ballet, *Giselle*, was first staged in Paris in 1841. It was the work of two French-trained choreographers, Jean Coralli and Jules Perrot, and it too has a sad story.

Giselle is a young peasant girl who lives in a cottage on the edge of the forest. She has fallen in love with Loys, whom she believes to be a village boy, but he is really the Duke Albrecht in disguise. Of course he wouldn't dream of marrying a simple village girl, and he is already engaged to a Princess. Hilarion, a gamekeeper, discovers the truth and tries to warn Giselle but, like any girl in love, she doesn't want to hear anything bad about her lover. However the truth comes out when some of Albrecht's friends arrive, and with them his fiancée, Bathilde. They are charmed by Giselle, and watch the ceremony in which she is crowned Queen of the Grape Harvest. At this moment Hilarion reveals Loys' true identity. Bathilde, who has been resting in Giselle's cottage, comes out to see what all the fuss is about, and claims Loys as her fiancé Albrecht. Giselle is so distressed that her mind gives way. She can no longer face reality and, brokenhearted, she tries desperately to recapture her former happiness by dancing again the joyful dances she once shared with Loys. At last, completely exhausted, she dies (in some productions she stabs herself with Albrecht's sword).

The second act takes place at Giselle's tomb in the forest. There her spirit is summoned to join the Wilis, who are led by their Queen, Myrtha. These are the spirits of young girls who have died before their wedding-day because they were betrayed by their lovers, and any man who sees them is forced to dance until he dies. Both Hilarion and Albrecht come to ask Giselle to forgive them. The Wilis soon drive Hilarion to his death, but Giselle cannot bear to see Albrecht punished. She realises that he has suffered, that his grief is genuine, and that she still loves him. Myrtha commands Giselle to make Albrecht dance to his death, but Giselle is too tender-hearted. She tells him that he will be protected by the cross on her grave, and she dances for him until dawn, when the power of the Wilis comes to an end. Thus he is saved by her love and forgiveness.

As you can see from the story, Giselle is a wonderful role that demands a superb dancer and a great actress. She has to convey a wide range of feelings, from the joy and happiness of being in love to the depth of a grief that causes madness, and she has to make the change from a carefree country girl into a spirit from another world – someone who can still feel love but is also an unearthly being, and a little frightening as all ghosts are. Anna Pavlova's mad-scene was much admired, and when she repeated the lively dances Giselle had done when she was happy, she danced slowly and made them seem like memories that had become broken and jumbled up in her mind. She was so moving that the other dancers sometimes cried when she 'died', and she thought herself into the part with such intensity that she lived rather than acted it.

Another famous Giselle, Margot Fonteyn, emphasised Giselle's feeling of being betrayed by the very people she had been brought up to honour and trust – the aristocracy represented by Albrecht and his fiancée – and made this one of the things that drove her mad. A more recent Giselle, Antoinette Sibley, says it is her favourite classical role and one she finds very easy to understand. '. . . I know what it feels like not to be strong and healthy – and also to fall hopelessly in love and believe everything that I'm told. For anybody who believes so totally, the deception when discovered can break their heart. It is not a fairy story, like *Sleeping Beauty*, it is something real about grief and loss and love.'

There are different ways of looking at Albrecht too. Nureyev brought to the role the Russian view of him as a thoughtless young aristocrat who is later overcome with remorse, while Anthony Dowell plays the first act for real. 'I did "believe" I was in love with Giselle; and when I was shown up at the end of act one, it was one of those unpleasant tricks life plays on people who are leading double lives but refuse to recognise it: everything turns horribly nasty in a sudden traumatic shock.'

Each production of *Giselle* (and there have been many since Diaghilev first revived it in 1910) has found something new to say about the characters. There is no one way of playing Giselle or Albrecht, and this is part of their fascination. Famous Giselles of recent years include the Russians Ekaterina Maximova (who was coached by Ulanova), and Natalia Makarova, Marcia Haydée and Eva Evdokimova.

Everyone knows the fairy-tale of the Sleeping Beauty, but it isn't the ideal plot for a full-length ballet. The characters have no depth and can easily seem like cardboard figures, and the action is all over before the last act, yet by some magic this is one of the most beautiful and splendid ballets. It was dreamed up by Ivan Vsevolozhsky, Director of the Russian Imperial Theatres at the end of the nineteenth century. He loved Tchaikowsky's music and was eager to commission him to write a ballet. He wanted it set in the period of the French king Louis XIV, so that he could order very extravagant sets and costumes, and he wanted a finale that included lots of other fairy-tale characters. In fact there were to be lots of the kind of dances that did nothing for the plot but showed off the dazzling tricks of the dancers, because this was what the audiences of the time loved.

He decided to start with a prologue showing the christening of the baby Princess. Six fairies arrive with their partners and each dances a solo before giving the baby her gift. Suddenly they are interrupted by the wicked fairy Carabosse, who is furious at not being invited and brings a most unwelcome gift: one day the Princess will prick her finger and die. But the Lilac Fairy has not yet given her present, and she saves the situation. She promises that the Princess will not die, but fall into a deep sleep from which she will be wakened by the kiss of a Prince.

Act I takes place on Princess Aurora's sixteenth birthday. A group of old women who have been caught knitting are condemned to death – no needles are allowed in the kingdom – but the Queen arranges a pardon for them as it is such a special day. Four Princes arrive to woo Aurora, and she dances a sparkling solo full of show-off balancing acts with each of them. Suddenly an old woman offers her a surprise present – a spindle – and before her parents can stop her, Aurora has pricked her finger on it. She tries to dance on, but slowly falls asleep. The old woman throws back her cloak. It is Carabosse, and she vanishes in a puff of smoke. The court is horrified, but the Lilac Fairy appears and casts a spell over the palace. Aurora is borne away to her bedroom, the King, the Queen and the courtiers fall asleep, and a forest springs up round the palace.

In Act II it is a hundred years later. Prince Florimund is out hunting when suddenly the Lilac Fairy appears. She tells him about the sleeping Princess and shows him a vision of her. Aurora looks so beautiful that he at once falls in love with her and begs the Fairy to lead him to the palace. They journey through the magic forest, and the Prince walks straight through the sleeping palace to Aurora's bedroom. He wakens her with a kiss, and at once everyone else comes back to life.

Act III celebrates the wedding of the Prince and Princess, and it is such a feast of dancing that it is sometimes performed on its own under the title *Aurora's Wedding*. It is one big party, with some unusual guests such as Puss-in-Boots and the White Cat, Red Riding Hood and the Wolf, and Cinderella and her Prince. They don't all appear in every production, but there is one couple who are never left out – the Bluebird and his partner. The Bluebird dance is a dazzling male solo, and needs a dancer who can really jump and soar through the air. It is a thrilling example of elevation that displays the male dancer at his most brilliant. The ballet ends with everyone joining in a mazurka and presumably living happily ever after.

Vsevolozhsky sent his scenario to the ballet-master Marius Petipa, who was an expert at arranging this kind of grand spectacle. In a career lasting nearly sixty years he created fifty-seven new ballets – and this was to be his masterpiece. He went to work enthusiastically, and produced a detailed plan of the kind of music he wanted. He didn't just ask Tchaikowsky for lively music at one moment and 'tender, fantastic, and magical music' at another, but also specified how many bars would be needed and the speed at which the music should be played. When it was found that the music wouldn't stretch to cover the unrolling of a long piece of scenery, Tchaikowsky obligingly wrote a few more 'yards'. Far from upsetting the composer, he found the exact requirements very inspiring and wrote some of his finest ballet music for *The Sleeping Beauty*. It has a wonderful sense of a great occasion, and makes you feel that something very grand and special is happening, like a state occasion and a birthday rolled into one.

The ballet had a great effect on Diaghilev and all his friends. He longed to show off its splendour outside Russia, but when he staged it in London in 1921, it was an expensive flop. However, it was chosen by The Royal Ballet as their first production at Covent Garden, and today it is thought of as one of the stiffest tests of a company's dancing strength. As Anthony Dowell says, the story and the characters don't give dancers anything to hide behind. 'You just have to dance well and if you cannot, that is what shows; there is nothing to cover up any faulty technique . . .' Yet when it is danced by a great ballerina and a superb company, there are moments of pure magic when the audience is spellbound.

Swan Lake is now the most popular ballet in the world, but at first it was not at all successful, and it took nearly twenty years and new choreography to do final justice to Tchaikowsky's haunting, melancholy music.

The story is very romantic and presents love as a fateful experience that can only end in death. When it opens, Prince Siegfried is celebrating his birthday. His mother thinks it is time he got married, and has arranged a ball so that he can choose his bride, but Siegfried prefers to go hunting with his friends. They pursue a flock of swans, and when Siegfried catches up with the leader, she turns into a beautiful girl.

She tells him that her name is Odette, that she has been enchanted by a wicked sorcerer, von Rothbart, and that she can only be freed if a man will swear and keep an oath to love her and be faithful to her. And of course Siegfried is only too willing to make such a promise. That night at the ball his thoughts are full of Odette, and he has no time for any of the girls his mother has invited. But when von Rothbart arrives with his daughter Odile, who is disguised as Odette, Siegfried is deceived and rushes up to dance with her. Although the real Odette appears and tries to warn him, Siegfried doesn't notice her, and at the end of their dance he asks Odile to marry him. Then he realises that he has made a terrible mistake, and rushes off to find Odette.

Von Rothbart causes a storm to stop them from meeting, but Siegfried finds Odette and asks for her forgiveness. She has decided to drown herself in the lake, as now she will never be free, and Siegfried offers to join her. Their deaths destroy von Rothbart's power, and they are seen together at the bottom of the lake, united in eternal love.

When it was decided to revive *Swan Lake* after the great success of *The Sleeping Beauty*, Petipa arranged the dances for the court scenes and created some specially difficult solos for the Italian ballerina Pierina Legnani. She was famous for being able to perform thirty-two *fouettés*, one after the other – something no Russian dancer could do – and Petipa included these in the dance in which Odile dazzles Siegfried. (A *fouetté* is a step in which the dancer spins round on one toe, using the other leg to 'whip' her round as though she were a top.) The 'white' acts in which the swans appear were arranged by Petipa's assistant, Ivanov. As a contrast to Odile's dancing he created poetical, dreamlike dances that reflect the soft, fluttering movements of the swans. The same ballerina usually plays both Odette and Odile, and she has to seem fragile and romantic in the white acts and hard and glittering in the black act (so called because Odile traditionally wears black). It is a very testing part and calls for a superb technique and great acting.

There have been hundreds of performances and productions of *Swan Lake* since 1895, and from time to time new dances have been added and the music rearranged. The original *Swan Lake* is lost in the mists of time, but the nearest version to it is said to be that first danced by the Sadler's Wells Ballet in 1934 and still in their repertoire. This was staged with the help of notes smuggled out of Russia by a former manager of the Maryinsky Theatre. In the Soviet Union the Russians have now given the ballet a happy ending because they find it politically more acceptable, but if you listen to the music you will find it hard to believe that this is what Tchaikowsky intended.

The plot of *The Nutcracker* originally sounded more like a nightmare than a Christmas story. Its heroine, Clara, is a little girl who is given a Nutcracker doll by an eccentric old man, Herr Drosselmeyer. She falls asleep after a Christmas party and dreams that a fight has broken out between some mice and her brother's toy soldiers, led by the Nutcracker doll. When Clara saves his life, he turns into a handsome prince and takes her on a journey to the Kingdom of Sweets. They travel through a snow-covered forest peopled by dancing snowflakes, and when they reach the Kingdom of Sweets, they are welcomed by the Sugar Plum Fairy. There is a special programme of dances in Clara's honour, including Spanish, Arabian, Chinese and Russian dances, a *pas de deux* for the Sugar Plum Fairy, and an irresistible waltz for the flowers.

The first performance in 1892 was a failure – the critics were very rude about it – and there have been many attempts to improve the rather weak story. In his version Nureyev makes Herr Drosselmeyer turn into the Prince, and gives the plot a psychological twist so that Clara grows up in her dream and becomes the Prince's partner. He also brings back some of the nastiness of the original fairy-tale, as his mice are really horrid. But whatever the changes, *The Nutcracker* always pops up at Christmas and is a great favourite, partly because of the very descriptive, sparkling music. Tchaikowsky didn't like the plot and complained that it was impossible to write about the Kingdom of Sweets, but if you know the little tinkling dance of the Sugar Plum Fairy, written for a new instrument, the celeste, you will see how brilliantly he accomplished his trying task.

Most audiences prefer the story-ballets, but there is one short, plotless ballet that is just as famous as *Swan Lake*. It was originally called *Chopiniana* in honour of its music, which is by Chopin, and it is still called this in the Soviet Union, but elsewhere it is known as *Les Sylphides* – the title suggested by Benois when Diaghilev took the ballet to Paris in 1909.

It took Fokine only three days to create the ballet, and although the mood and the dancers' long white dresses look back to the Romantic period, it is full of Fokine's new ideas. Those taking part included Nijinsky, Pavlova and Karsavina, but the dances are not show-off pieces. Instead, the solos are woven together to create a feeling of sadness and wistful longing that works in the same way as a poem. The one male dancer could be thought of as Chopin or a poet dancing with his dreams – it is not important. What matters is that the audience should be caught up in the dream and able to enjoy its romantic nature. If the ballet doesn't cast this spell, then it doesn't work, but don't worry if you're not carried away, and don't ask it to tell you something about life today. Instead, try to respond to the music, the beautiful patterns formed by the dancers, and the romantic mood.

All the ballets in this chapter so far have proved their staying power by lasting for years, but although *La Fille Mal Gardée* has an old story, it was made into a brand new ballet by Frederick Ashton in 1960. It is a country tale about a girl called Lise who is in love with a young farmer, but whose mother wants her to marry a very stupid young man because he is rich. The title (which sounds much better in French than in English) refers to the fact that however hard her mother tries to keep an eye on Lise, she can't stop her meeting her boyfriend. They flirt and dance together despite all mother's precautions, and finally manage to get locked in the bedroom. When they are discovered, the rich young man's father tears up the marriage contract, and the young couple are free to marry.

It's a real country story that just has to have a happy ending. It starts with a brilliant dance by the farmyard cock and his harem of hens, and then Lise's mother (always danced by a man) continues the comedy. She is a glorified pantomime dame who throws things at the hero, chases her daughter, and does a superb clog dance. The silly young man is a comedian too. He is very attached to his lovely red umbrella, and he is so dim that he has no idea how to court Lise. Everyone makes fun of him, but the teasing is good-natured because it is too sunny a ballet for anyone to get hurt.

As always, Ashton finds just the right steps for love. The young couple have a delightful *pas de deux* in which they play with a length of ribbon, letting it bind them together and then twisting it into a giant cat's cradle. When the villagers come home from the harvest, they set up a maypole and weave the ribbons into patterns of happiness. Even the sudden rainstorm doesn't dampen the high spirits, but simply adds the English weather to a charming picture of country life as we all like to think it was once upon a time. The Royal Ballet production includes a barrel-shaped Shetland pony, who isn't quite up to dancing but seems to enjoy pulling a cart. And in true animal fashion, it gets all the attention while on stage!

Of course there are lots of other marvellous ballets (and you can find out about them from *Ballet for All* by Peter Brinson and Clement Crisp), but many of them are not being danced at the moment, whereas the ones described here are always being danced by companies in Britain and all over the world, so it shouldn't be too difficult to see them.

These ballets also turn up on television sometimes, though this isn't the best way to see them for the first time, because ballet seems so much more exciting live. But there have been some fascinating programmes about Diaghilev, Pavlova, Nijinsky, Marie Rambert, Ninette de Valois and Anthony Dowell, which give a real insight into the problems and rewards of dancers' lives.

The Royal Ballet have made several films, and this is one way of seeing Margot Fonteyn at her best, but the film to keep a special lookout for is *The Tales of Beatrix Potter*. Here the camera has used a special magic not possible on stage, and if Mrs Tiggy Winkle and Jeremy Fisher and all the other Beatrix Potter animals ever danced, it was surely just as Sir Frederick Ashton has imagined them.

8. Some famous companies

The goal of all dancers once they have finished their training is to join a company. It may sound a very glamorous way of earning a living, but it is also very hard work. In a typical working day, a dancer may have to fit in a practice class, a rehearsal for a new part, a session with a choreographer trying to work out a new ballet, and perhaps a visit to the wardrobe, before dashing off to the theatre for the evening's performance. And dancing a major role can be utterly exhausting. Dancers worry themselves sick about new parts, about failing, about not being able to master a certain step, and they are often terrified before a performance. What the audience never realises is that Juliet or Princess Aurora may be saying to herself, 'I can't do another step, I'll never get through it,' but top dancers often feel just like this.

Most companies go on tour, both in their own countries and abroad. As well as the obvious excitement of dancing at the Metropolitan in New York or La Scala, Milan, they often find themselves in small, out-of-the-way places with stages that are not at all suitable for ballet. Some dancers, especially Nureyev, hate travelling by air, and long journeys, bad digs, crowded dressing-rooms and slippery stages can soon take the shine off the joys of touring. Julian Braunsweg's *Ballet Scandals* is a very funny account of his adventures touring with the Festival Ballet. According to him, life behind the scenes crackles with quarrels, tempers and jealousies, and a gentle Giselle is capable of causing havoc because she doesn't like her dressing-room or feels she is not being given star treatment.

As we have seen, in the early days, ballet in Britain meant the Sadler's Wells Ballet and the Ballet Rambert. After the war, the Sadler's Wells Ballet started a second company known today as the Sadler's Wells Royal Ballet. It has its own dancers, some of them former members of the Covent Garden company, and dances ballets by Ashton, Balanchine, Cranko, de Valois, and such full-length favourites as *Coppelia* and *La Fille Mal Gardée*. You have a good chance of seeing them, as they are on tour much of the time. The Royal Ballet goes on tour too, but it usually appears at Covent Garden, and it is not always easy to get tickets. It is the international showcase of British ballet, and its programme includes splendid productions of the classics, new ballets, and some of the best ballets of the last few years. Ballet for All, the third company, is not so well known, though it reaches much wider audiences through community centres, festivals, small theatres and schools. Its ballet-plays, such as *The World of Giselle*, *Tchaikowsky and his Ballets* and *The Birth of The Royal Ballet* illustrate the history of ballet and introduce some of its aspects today. So if you're really keen on ballet and want to learn more about it, this is a marvellous way to start. (You can find out when and where the company is appearing from magazines such as *Dance and Dancers*.)

Apart from the Ballet Rambert, two other important British companies have sprung up since the war. The London Festival Ballet was called after the Festival of Britain, which took place soon after the company was formed in 1950. The idea grew out of a series of gala performances by Alicia Markova and Anton Dolin, and the lively impresario Julian Braunsweg raised the money and took on the job of running the company. One of his brightest ideas was to arrange for the company to dance at the Royal Festival Hall, which has since become its main London home. Braunsweg wanted to introduce ballet to as many people as possible and give them a chance to see international stars, so he engaged dancers such as Alexandra Danilova, Yvette Chauviré, Tamara Toumanova and Leonide Massine as guest soloists. Today the company has attracted many fine dancers as its principals, but there is still a welcome for stars like Patrice Bart from the Paris Opéra Ballet and Nureyev, who is everyone's guest and brought the Festival Ballet his production of *The Sleeping Beauty*.

The present Artistic Director, Beryl Grey, studied at the Sadler's Wells Ballet School and was a star pupil, dancing solos when she was only fifteen. She became a *prima ballerina*, danced all over the world (she was the first British ballerina to dance with the Bolshoi), and took over the London Festival Ballet in 1968. She found that audiences liked the full-length classics best, and today you can see the company in *Coppelia*, *Don Quixote*, *Giselle*, *The Sleeping Beauty*, *The Nutcracker* and *Swan Lake*. The company has also revived some of the Diaghilev ballets by Fokine and Massine, which gives you a chance to see them as something more than past history. They also like to stage new ballets, and one of their most successful has been Barry Moreland's *Prodigal Son*, danced to the catchy, ragtime music of Scott Joplin. Another success which is still very popular was Jack Carter's *The Witch Boy* (1956), first danced by John Gilpin, who was one of the company's early stars. Although the Festival Ballet is in a sense a rival of The Royal Ballet, the two companies have links through their dancers. Their latest choreographer, Ronald Hynd, and current stars Patricia Ruanne and Nicholas Johnson used to dance with The Royal Ballet.

As its name suggests, The Scottish Ballet spends much of its time in Scotland, but it also tours England and has danced in Paris, Australia and New Zealand. It started life as the Western Theatre Ballet, a small company creating new ballets about life today, and its aim was to introduce ballet to audiences outside London who didn't often have the chance to see dance companies. This was partly the idea of ex-Sadler's Wells dancer Peter Darrell. He started off liking fairy-tale ballets, but he came to feel that it was hard for modern audiences to become involved in them. He wanted them to feel that ballet was not just something in the past, but that it had vital links with life today. So he created a ballet called *Mods and Rockers* (1963), which was danced to the music of the Beatles. He studied their dance steps and got a Mod to advise him about the right clothes and behaviour. The result was fun. It attracted people who hadn't thought that ballet had any connection with their lives – and they stayed to see what else was in store.

Although The Scottish Ballet still does lots of new ballets, it is now big enough and successful enough to put on its own versions of the classics. It has enchanting productions of *Giselle* and *La Sylphide*, a very popular Christmas *Nutcracker*, a spectacular *Tales of Hoffmann*, and a new *Swan Lake*, staged to celebrate the ballet's hundredth birthday. Revivals include Fokine's *Le Carnaval*, a mixture of laughter and tears with Harlequin, Columbine and Pierrot, and Andrée Howard's *La Fête Etrange*. The company has attracted international stars as guest artists, and its Principals include Elaine McDonald, Graham Bart, Patricia Ruanne, Patricia Merrin, Andrea Durant and Noriko Ohara.

Two of the most famous ballet companies in the world are not often seen away from home. As you may have guessed, they are the great Russian companies, the Bolshoi and the Kirov. The Bolshoi Ballet (the word *bolshoi* is Russian for great) takes its name from the Bolshoi Theatre, but there was ballet in Moscow long before the present theatre was built in 1856. During the reign of the tsars the company took second place to the ballet at St Petersburg, but after the Revolution, when Moscow became the new capital, every effort was made to build it into the finest company in the Soviet Union. Many dancers were brought from the Kirov, including their great ballerina Galina Ulanova, famous for her performances as Giselle and as Juliet in *Romeo and Juliet* (1940) – one of the few fine ballets created since the Revolution. Present stars include Ekaterina Maximova and her husband Vladimir Vasiliev, Natalia Bessmertnova, and Mikhail Lavrovsky. The company occasionally visits London, and if you ever get the chance to see them, do go.

The Kirov Ballet of Leningrad has an even greater tradition, and in the days of the tsars it attracted some of the finest dancers and ballet-masters in the world. This was the company that inspired Diaghilev, and it is still the home of the purest classical style, which reflects the superb teaching of Agrippina Vaganova. She had a great influence on male dancing, and turned out pupils who could literally soar through the air thanks to their strong backs. The Kirov still produces great dancers, but it isn't always able to hold on to them, and Rudolf Nureyev, Natalia Makarova and Mikhail Baryshnikov have all left to dance in the West.

It is difficult to judge Russian ballet today as the companies aren't often seen in the West, but the general impression seems to be that although their technique is amazing, the ballets themselves are disappointing and often spoilt by their political message.

Ballet is still quite a newcomer in the United States, and their major contribution has been as the pioneer of modern dance. This began as a protest against the restrictions of classical ballet, and was inspired by Isadora Duncan, who preferred spontaneous movements and liked to dance barefoot. Her ideas were shared by dance-teacher Ruth St Denis and her husband Ted Shawn, and they had a great influence on Martha Graham, who formed a company to stage her breakaway ballets, and became the most important figure in the modern dance movement. Martha Graham has many followers, including the London Contemporary Dance Theatre.

Meanwhile classical ballet in the U.S.A. blossomed in two marvellous companies – the American Ballet Theater and the New York City Ballet. The American Ballet Theater has produced an American style that consists of a strict classical training pepped up with typical American vitality. The company started in 1939 and has strong European roots. Fokine staged his ballets for them, Antony Tudor brought his Rambert successes and added some brilliant new ballets, and guests included Markova, Dolin and Massine. They also put on *Fancy Free* (1944), the first ballet by America's leading choreographer, Jerome Robbins.

The first artistic director of the New York City Ballet was George Balanchine, and he created some of his best ballets for the company. The other great influence on this company has been Jerome Robbins, who created ten new ballets during his years with the company and later returned to produce the joyous *Dances at a Gathering*. He has helped to give classical ballet a modern flavour.

The oldest ballet company in the world is the Royal Danish Ballet, which was founded in 1748. During the nineteenth century it was made famous by the ballets of August Bournonville, which were the only Romantic ballets to have good parts for male dancers. During the 1930s and 40s, Harald Lander brought new life to the company and created many new ballets for it, and both

Fokine and Balanchine were guest choreographers. The fine Russian teacher Vera Volkova, a pupil of Vaganova, has since taught the Russian style of dancing, and the company now has a great reputation.

The influence of Britain's Royal Ballet is worldwide, and both Australia and Canada have national companies built up by former Sadler's Wells dancers in the best Ninette de Valois tradition. The Australian Ballet, founded in 1962, was for many years directed by Peggy Van Praagh, assisted by Robert Helpmann, who also did some choreography. Nureyev has danced with the company and they took part in his film *Don Quixote* – a lively, colourful record of a spirited production and his best film so far. The National Ballet of Canada was founded by Celia Franca in 1951. Its repertoire includes the classics, and ballets by Ashton, Balanchine, Tudor, John Neumeier and other modern choreographers. Top dancers are regular guests, and Nureyev did a special production of *The Sleeping Beauty* for this company. The other leading Canadian company, The Royal Winnipeg Ballet, was the first British company to gain the title 'Royal'. It concentrates on more experimental ballets, and is one of the few companies that still performs Kurt Jooss's *The Green Table* (1932), a famous political satire that makes fun of an international conference and shows how stupidly the delegates behave.

Of course there are many more ballet companies all over the world and new ones are springing up all the time, such as the Nederlands Dans Theater in Holland, which is bursting with ideas and puts on about ten new ballets a year by very modern choreographers such as Hans van Manen and Rudi van Dantzig. But there is space enough for only one more company which really can't be left out as it has rapidly become one of the finest in the world. There was ballet in Stuttgart as far back as the eighteenth century, but it was not until the 1960s, under the directorship of John Cranko, that the company became really famous. Cranko built it up by bringing in star dancers, training his own students and sending them to the Royal Ballet School, and by creating no less than fifty superb new ballets in the dozen years until his death. Now the company is run by his greatest star, Marcia Haydée, who has gone on commissioning new works, notably by

Glen Tetley and Kenneth MacMillan. The company dances Cranko's ballets better than anyone else (and that includes The Royal Ballet), and has a marvellous strength and vitality that is tremendously exciting.

Although some of the companies mentioned may seem far away, most of them have visited London in the last few years. If you do get the chance to see them, grab it, no matter what they are dancing. This is your chance to make discoveries and to learn firsthand about different styles of dancing. Then one day you will no longer need to read about the differences between Russian, English or Stuttgart dancers, because you will have spotted them yourself.

9 · Who's dancing?

Once you become involved in ballet, you soon find you have favourite dancers and are ready to queue up to see them dance. The mere fact that you've noticed them means that they must have personality, which is at least half-way to becoming a star, and probably many of the other qualities described in Chapter 2.

All the dancers listed here are stars or have come part of the way to stardom. They are all principal dancers, which means that they dance leading roles. Most belong to British companies or appear as their guests. (The Royal Ballet has been shortened to The R.B.)

Ashmole, David Born in Yorkshire, studied at the R.B. School, joined The R.B. in 1968, and is now a principal with the Sadler's Wells company. A promising young dancer with elegant looks and a soft lyrical style, David was soon dancing the prince in the big classical ballets. Look out for him also as the young farmer in *La Fille Mal Gardée* and Franz in *Coppelia*.

Barbieri, Margaret Born in South Africa, said to be a great-niece of the famous teacher Cecchetti, studied at the R.B. School and joined the Sadler's Wells company in 1965. Scored a great success as Giselle at the age of twenty-one, when she took over the part at Covent Garden at short notice, and has danced it in Berlin, Durban, Norway and Prague. A charming romantic dancer, she is also good at character parts such as the spiteful sister in MacMillan's *Las Hermanas*. See her as Swanhilda in *Coppelia*, Lise in *La Fille Mal Gardée*, and the Girl in *The Two Pigeons*.

Bart, Graham Born in Gloucester, trained at the Rambert and R.B. schools. Spent five years with the Sadler's Wells company and joined The Scottish Ballet in 1974. Dances leading roles in all the company's full-length ballets, and partnered Margot Fonteyn when she appeared with them. Married to Andrea Durant, another principal of the company.

Bart, Patrice French dancer who is a regular guest of the London Festival Ballet. Studied at the Paris Opéra School, joined the company at fourteen, and is now one of their leading dancers. Was invited to dance with the Bolshoi and Kirov companies and was a great success in *Giselle* and *Swan Lake*. Toured Australia with the Royal Winnipeg Ballet. Dances all the major classical roles.

Coleman, Michael Born in Scotland, studied at R.B. School, joined The R.B. touring company in 1959 and became a principal at Covent Garden in 1969. Best in virtuoso roles like Colas in *La Fille Mal Gardée* and comic ballets such as *Elite Syncopations* and *The Concert*. A splendid Jeremy Fisher in *The Tales of Beatrix Potter*.

Collier, Lesley Born in Kent, began dancing at the age of two, went to the R.B. School at eleven and joined The R.B. in 1965. Danced Lise in *La Fille Mal Gardée* in 1970, a role that suits her sparkling personality, and showed she could act too when she took over the title-role in *Anastasia*. She has now danced the lead in all the great classical ballets and is fast becoming a star. Was one of the Two Bad Mice in the film *The Tales of Beatrix Potter*.

Cragun, Richard American dancer who studied in Canada, at the R.B. School, and in Denmark. In 1962 joined the *corps de ballet* of the Stuttgart Ballet and soon became one of their leading dancers. Created leading roles in many Cranko ballets including the virile Petrucchio in *The Taming of the Shrew*. Cragun claims to have Indian blood in his veins. Perhaps this is why he is a very masculine dancer, displaying all the strength and grace of a superb athlete.

Dowell, Anthony Born in London, spent eight years at the R.B. School, joined the Covent Garden Opera Ballet in 1961 and The R.B. a year later. In 1964 Ashton chose him to create the role of Oberon in *The Dream*, and this was the beginning of a marvellous partnership with Antoinette Sibley. They have danced all the major classics together, and many short works such as *Symphonic Variations* and *La Bayadère*. Dowell has a brilliant technique, a lovely lyrical style, and is very good at breathing life into conventional heroes such as Albrecht in *Giselle*, Prince Siegfried in *Swan Lake*, and Prince Florimund in *The Sleeping Beauty*. His good looks and natural acting make him an outstanding Romeo. He has created roles in a variety of new ballets, the most recent being the young tutor in *A Month in the Country*. Dowell is the finest male dancer The R.B. has produced so far – and the youngest dancer ever to be awarded the CBE.

Eagling, Wayne Born in Canada, studied at the R.B. School, and joined The R.B. in 1969. Created his first role, the Brother in MacMillan's *Triad* (1972), while still in the *corps de ballet*. In 1973 danced Romeo to Lesley Collier's Juliet, and in 1974 took over Dowell's role in MacMillan's *Manon* and danced his first Prince Siegfried. He is one of the most gifted younger dancers. Notice his good line and splendid jumps.

Evdokimova, Eva Her father is Bulgarian, her mother Canadian, and she was born in Switzerland, so she is a truly international dancer. Studied at the Munich Opera Ballet and the R.B. School. Joined The Royal Danish Ballet at seventeen, and then returned to Germany to become *prima ballerina* of the Deutsch Oper in Berlin. In 1970 danced with the Kirov, and won a gold medal at the Varna Festival in Bulgaria. She is a beautiful Giselle, but says that her favourite role is Juliet. She often dances the major classics with the London Festival Ballet.

Fonteyn, Margot The greatest ballerina produced by The R.B., she still makes guest appearances with them and with many other companies all over the world. Studied with various teachers and at the Sadler's Wells Ballet School (see Chapter 2). Made her first appearance with the Vic-Wells Ballet as a Snowflake in *The Nut-cracker* in 1934, and was soon promoted to leading roles. Her beautiful line and musicality shone in the great classical ballets, and her special relationship with Ashton inspired many new ballets from *Le Baiser de la Fée* in 1935 down to *Marguerite and Armand* nearly thirty years later. In 1962 she befriended the young Russian dancer Rudolph Nureyev, and they soon formed a partnership that brought fresh distinction to her already glittering career. She was awarded the DBE, and is now Dame Margot. Fonteyn also hit the headlines with her marriage to Panamanian diplomat Tito Arias, who was later shot and badly wounded, and you can read about her unusual marriage and her life as a dancer in her autobiography, published in 1975.

Gielgud, Maina A member of a famous theatrical family (Sir John Gielgud is her uncle), she sees herself as an actress-ballerina. She studied in England, France and all over the world with many famous teachers, and danced with various companies in France. There met revolutionary French dancer/choreographer Maurice Béjart, who invited her to join his Ballet of the 20th Century. She loved his modern ballets and found them 'really relevant to today'. From 1972–5 danced many classical and modern roles with the London Festival Ballet, and in 1976–7 was a guest of the Sadler's Wells Royal Ballet. Loves Juliet in the Cranko ballet and has danced this with the Australian Ballet.

Haydée, Marcia Brazilian dancer who is Artistic Director and *prima ballerina* of the Stuttgart Ballet. Won a scholarship to the R.B. School in 1954, joined the Marquis de Cuevas Ballet in 1956, and spent four years with them. Went to the Stuttgart Ballet in 1961, and inspired Cranko to create some wonderful roles for her. Glen Tetley and Kenneth MacMillan have also produced ballets specially for her. She is a brilliant classical dancer, and has been the guest of The Royal Ballet, the American Ballet Theater and the Canadian National Ballet.

Kelly, Desmond Born in Southern Rhodesia. Danced with the London Festival Ballet, the Zurich Ballet, the New Zealand Ballet and the National Ballet of Washington, before joining The R.B. in 1970. A handsome, brilliant partner, he has been very successful in the great classical ballets and danced with many leading ballerinas including Margot Fonteyn. Some of his best roles are the Husband in MacMillan's *The Invitation*, and the title-roles in *Apollo* and *The Prodigal Son*. He recently spent some time touring with the Sadler's Wells company, and danced in *La Fille Mal Gardée*, *Coppelia*, *The Two Pigeons* and *The Lady and the Fool*.

Madsen, Egon Danish dancer who studied with Vera Volkova and John Cranko. Joined the Stuttgart Ballet in 1961, and created roles in many Cranko ballets. A brilliant, stylish, witty dancer who can also be deeply moving and poetic. Has made guest appearances with both The R.B. companies.

Makarova, Natalia Russian dancer who trained at the Leningrad Ballet School and joined the Kirov Ballet in 1959. A superb classical dancer, she ran away from the Kirov in 1970, while they were appearing in London, and asked for political asylum. Later that year she joined the American Ballet Theater, and has since danced the great classical ballets as the guest of many companies including The R.B. She has a touching fragility on stage, and is one of the finest Giselles of recent years.

McDonald, Elaine Born in Yorkshire and began her training at the R.B. School. Has been with the Scottish Ballet since it was formed in 1969, and danced all the leading roles. Look out for her Giselle, which has been much praised. Peter Darrell has created many roles for her, including the title-role in his *Mary Queen of Scots* (1976).

Mason, Monica Born in Johannesburg, she joined The R.B. when she was only sixteen. Her first role was created for her – the Chosen Maiden in MacMillan's *The Rite of Spring*, in 1962. She has a strong technique, a warm personality, and natural dramatic sense. She excels in classical roles such as Odette/Odile, Princess Aurora and Giselle, and in dramatic parts, and MacMillan has created several roles for her.

Nureyev, Rudolf Russian dancer who leapt to fame in the West when he left the Kirov Ballet while dancing in Paris in 1961. He studied at the Leningrad Ballet School after a determined battle to become a dancer (see Chapter 2). He joined the Kirov in 1958, and was soon partnering their top ballerinas. His career in the West began with the Marquis de Cuevas Ballet, and then in 1962 he made a spectacular début at Covent Garden in *Giselle*. This was the start of a legendary partnership with Margot Fonteyn, and at the end of the evening they took twenty-three curtain calls. Nureyev has now danced more than eighty roles with thirty different companies, and has also staged nineteen productions including *The Nutcracker*, *Raymonda*, *The Sleeping Beauty*, *Swan Lake*, *La Bayadère* and *Don Quixote*, which feature new dances arranged by him. He has appeared in five films including *An Evening with The Royal Ballet* (in which he danced his exciting *Le Corsair* and *Les Sylphides*), *Don Quixote* with the Australian Ballet, and the documentary *I am a Dancer*. Nureyev is famous for his magnetic personality, his thrilling technique and elevation, and his inexhaustible energy. In 1976 he staged a Nureyev Festival at which he danced every night for seven weeks – and insisted on continuing even with an injury. His autobiography, published in 1962, shows him as a dashing young dancer, and *The Nureyev Image* by Alexander Bland and *Nureyev* by John Percival will tell you more about why he is such a great dancer.

Park, Merle Born in Rhodesia, studied in England, and joined The R.B. in 1954. She has a superb technique and a strong musical sense, and has danced all the great classical ballets and contemporary works such as *Romeo and Juliet*, *La Fille Mal Gardée*, *Manon* and *Cinderella*. Her sparkling personality is at its best in lighthearted roles, and she was a great success as Swanhilda in *Coppelia* in 1975. She often dances with Nureyev, and appeared in a six-week Broadway season of *Nureyev and Friends* in 1975. Her guest appearances have taken her all over the world, and in 1975 she danced in Brazil with the Ballet de Rio de Janeiro. She was awarded the CBE in 1974.

Parkinson, Georgina Born in Brighton, studied at the R.B. School, joined The R.B. in 1955. Created the title-role in Andrée Howard's *La Belle Dame Sans Merci* in 1959, and went on to make her mark with her classical technique and strong dramatic sense. Juliet is one of her finest roles, but nowadays she plays Lady Capulet. She is also a beautiful and dignified Tsarina in *Anastasia*.

Penney, Jennifer Born in Vancouver, studied with the founders of the Royal Winnipeg Ballet and at the R.B. School, and joined The R.B. in 1963. Danced her first major roles while still in the *corps de ballet*, and was praised for her pure classical technique. Was a great success as Princess Aurora in 1968. MacMillan has created several roles for her, and chose her to succeed Sibley in the difficult part of Manon. She is one of the most promising young ballerinas, and recent roles have included parts in *Symphonic Variations* and *Dances at a Gathering*.

Prokovsky, André French dancer who made his debut in 1954. Became a leading dancer with the London Festival Ballet in 1958, then left to dance with the Marquis de Cuevas Ballet and the New York City Ballet, returning to the Festival Ballet as principal dancer in 1967. Left with his partner Galina Samsova to found the New London Ballet in 1972. A fine classical dancer who often makes guest appearances with other companies.

Ruanne, Patricia Born in Leeds, trained at the R.B. School and joined The R.B. when she was seventeen. Later joined the Sadler's Wells company and danced in a variety of modern ballets put on by their New Group. In 1973 joined the London Festival Ballet and has danced all the classics with them, including Princess Aurora in Nureyev's new production of *The Sleeping Beauty*. Two of her most exciting roles have been the sexy Siren in *Prodigal Son* (in *Ragtime*), and the Queen of Shemakhan in the 1976 revival of the spectacular *Le Coq d'Or*.

Samsova, Galina Russian dancer who studied at the Kiev Choreography School and then joined the Kiev Opera and Ballet Theatre. Came to the West, danced with the National Ballet of Canada, and then joined the London Festival Ballet in 1964. With

André Prokovsky as her partner, she became *prima ballerina* and graced their productions of the major classics. In 1972 she founded the New London Ballet with Prokovsky, and often makes guest appearances with other companies.

Seymour, Lynn Born in Canada, trained at the R.B. School and joined The R.B. in 1957. In her first year created her first major role (the Adolescent in MacMillan's *The Burrow*), and danced *Swan Lake* and *Giselle*. In 1966 she left to dance with the Deutsche Oper in Berlin, but returned to The R.B. in 1970. She is a very dramatic dancer, and this quality inspired MacMillan to create many roles for her, including Juliet and Anastasia. Her zany sense of humour suits the Jerome Robbins' ballets *Dances at a Gathering* and *The Concert*, and she was a stormy and moving Kate in Cranko's *The Taming of the Shrew*. She has been a guest artist of many companies, and recently tried her hand at choreography. In 1976 she danced her first *Manon*, created the role of Natalia Petrovna in *A Month in the Country*, was awarded the CBE, and won the Evening Standard Ballet award for the year's outstanding contribution to dancing.

Sibley, Antoinette Born in Kent, studied at the R.B. School and joined The R.B. in 1956. Made her mark in 1959, when she took over the lead in *Swan Lake* at short notice. Has become famous for her interpretations of the great classical roles, in which she usually dances with Anthony Dowell. Their partnership, which began with *The Dream* in 1964, also extends to short ballets, and is commemorated in the book *Sibley and Dowell* by Leslie Spatt and Nicholas Dromgoole, which has many marvellous photographs of them. She was awarded the CBE in 1973, and her dancing shows the English style at its classical best.

Sleep, Wayne Born in Plymouth, studied at the R.B. School, joined The R.B. in 1966. A small, lively, virtuoso dancer, he gets the maximum fun out of his lack of inches. He is particularly good as Puck in *The Dream*, the Gypsy Boy in *The Two Pigeons*, and Kolia, the small boy who rushes round the stage with his kite, in *A Month in the Country*. He has also appeared as an actor in various films and plays, and was one of the Two Bad Mice in the film *The Tales of Beatrix Potter*.

Wall, David Born in London, studied at the R.B. School and joined The R.B. touring company. While still in the *corps de ballet* he danced the leads in *Swan Lake* and *La Fille Mal Gardée* at Covent Garden. In 1966, at the age of twenty, he became the youngest principal in the history of the company, thanks to his brilliant technique and an attractive personality that brings the classical heroes to life. He has often danced with Fonteyn, and played all the major classical roles. His most important new role has been Lescaut in *Manon*, which showed a gift for comedy that also made his swaggering Petrucchio in Cranko's *The Taming of the Shrew* such fun.

Index

More Beaver Books

We hope you have enjoyed this Beaver Book. Here are some of the other titles:

Wild Lone 'BB's' classic depiction of the life of a fox in hunting countryside, for older readers. The author's book *The Lord of the Forest* is also available in Beavers

Storm Warning A powerful novel for older readers set in pre-War Nazi Germany, about a young English girl who helps two Jewish children escape from the Gestapo. By Mara Kay

Covens and Cauldrons An anthology of stories, folk tales, poems and legends about witches, edited by Jacynth Hope-Simpson and strikingly illustrated by Krystyna Turska.

The Beaver Book of Gadgets Harvey Weiss gives easy-to-follow instructions for making all sorts of gadgets including lamps, mobiles, games and even a burglar alarm! Fully illustrated with line drawings, for the nimble-fingered of nine upwards

The Beaver Book of Extra Money A Beaver original. Dozens of ideas for earning extra money in your spare time, from exercising dogs to helping out at children's parties. Humorous illustrations by Mik Brown accompany Merry Archard's lively text for readers of ten upwards

Making and Flying Kites How to make and fly sixteen different kites, from the traditional Hargrave box kite to the exciting Nagasaki fighting kite, by A. Lloyd, C. Mitchell and N. Thomas

New Beavers are published every month and if you would like the *Beaver Bulletin* – which gives all the details – please send a large stamped addressed envelope to:

Beaver Bulletin
The Hamlyn Group
Astronaut House
Feltham
Middlesex TW14 9AR

31412X